*C*rossing *O*ver

Ellie Collins Story

By: Ish Payne

Foreword By:
Jack W. Hayford

FOREWORD

Ellie …
I was so moved to read of the moment God's love became
tenderly & powerfully real to you.
That it occurred as He allowed my broadcast to bring that
truth & life to you is all the
more moving!
May He be glorified … Lord, may this story of yours
multiply the message of Jesus' reality & graciousness to
multitudes.
I believe "Crossing Over" is going to be a bridge from
death to life,
futility to hope,
and emptiness to fulfillment
for many!

Jack W. Hayford
Chancellor
The King's University

ENDORSEMENTS

There is not a human being on earth who is not broken in some way. Some of us are fractured internally and have found ways to mask our pain, while others have been so grievously injured, there's simply no disguise for the ache within our souls. Many of us have felt helpless at one point or another, but few "have walked through mine fields of depravity and manipulation" as Ellie did for the first 19 years of her life. All of us have been corrupted in some way, but very few have faced the defilement and abandonment Ellie lived in day in and day out for the first two decades of her life. In reading about her journey, we can easily recognize that our difficulties pale in comparison, so her testimony holds enormous promise for each of us! *"If God delivered her, can He not do the same for me?"* comes to mind...

By sharing Ellie's testimony and the knowledge he's accumulated over the years, Ish Payne has invited each one of us into healing. He has shown us what the Holy Spirit can do and proven that nothing is too difficult for God!

We do indeed serve a God of deliverance, who delights in rescuing and redeeming! Not only is **Crossing Over** a celebration of His goodness and grace, it also offers practical instruction on the powerful truths that set Ellie free, that can be applied anew in our own lives. This timely book has the promising potential to both edify and equip the body of Christ. I am delighted to have the honor of endorsing it!

Kathi Wilson
Christian Music Psalmist/Singer/Songwriter
(Kathi's songs are used in the book and Ellie
chose her song 'Crossing Over' for the title)
www.Living-Water-Productions.com

Ellie's life is truly a remarkable and heartwarming story of God's love and power to redeem the abused. Ellie, and her husband Randy are part of my church staff, and I can verify that the transformation described in these pages is true. Ish Payne retells this redemptive story in a God-honoring way that reminds all of us that God heals the broken and will do it for anyone who calls to Him.

If you like true stories about God helping the hopeless, you'll love *Crossing Over*!

Jerry Dirmann
Sr. Pastor, The Rock
Anaheim, California

When Ish relayed Ellie's tragic past to me, how she is thriving today, and that he was writing a book to help people get free and stay free, I knew it would be a book with HOPE stamped all over it.

I've ministered to brokenhearted people for 23 years and never heard a story of abuse this extreme! Ish lays out in simple to follow steps the process of forgiveness to freedom – Revelation – Redemption – Resolution – Reconciliation and Revival.

Every abused person needs to read this book! And every person who takes the mandate of Jesus seriously to set the captive free will learn many truths to walk with others as they are *Crossing Over*!

Deanne Day
Restoring Hearts, Inc
Team member Restoring Hearts Ministries
www.RestoringHearts.net

Not only is Ish Payne an incredible man of God, he's an anointed writer. In *Crossing Over*, Ish paints a beautiful portrait of God's redemption and healing through Ellie's story. It is a great testimony of God's love that penetrates the heart of the reader in a way that moves you closer to God's grace.

Ish outlines one of the best road maps of forgiveness I've ever seen, this practical biblical path leads to the foot of the cross.

I highly recommend this for anyone dealing with issues of Restoration, forgiveness, healing or redemption. I promise you it will transform your life in a fresh and powerful way!

Larry Brey
Associate Pastor
Elevation Church
Matthews, NC
www.ElevationChurch.org

CROSSING OVER

Copyright 2010
Restoring Hearts Ministries
PO Box 100
Indian Trail NC 28079

Printed in the United States of America
2nd Edition 2010

Type set, formatting, cover design and self-publishing:
Linda Lange
Life Application Ministries Publishing (LAMP)

P.O. Box 165
Mt. Aukum, CA 95656

Printer: createspace.com

To the Reader

Ish Payne
Restoring Hearts Ministries
PO Box 100
Indian Trail, NC 28079
www.Restoringhearts.net

ACKNOWLEDGEMENTS

To the many dear friends who have labored with me to see His kingdom come to earth – I love you dearly – without your help this book would not have been written. I know that God's eternal history will reveal that your love for the lost and dying, the lost ones who have been 'Restored' through **Crossing Over,** will be a beautiful stone in your crown of life!

My special thanks to the following people for their help in editing and proofing my manuscript:

- Tonda, my precious warrior wife!
- Taylor and Lexie, my sweet daughters! Thanks for the hints.
- Ann Wild, my mother in law – one special lady!
- Susie Fiske, thank you for your patient tenacity – you are awesome!
- Amanda Conrad & Laureen Jenkins – my dear friends!

To the Psalmist's who blessed us with their songs of love and grace. I wept many tears over these songs of redemption as I wrote while listening to your music – thank you for the powerful anointing of liberty to establish His Kingdom!

- Kathi Wilson ... *Living Water Productions, LLC*
- Deanne Day ... *Restoring Hearts, Inc*
- Chris Brown, Mack Brock, Wade Joye ... *Elevation Worship Publishing*
- Jan Marie Savoie ... *Jan Marie Savoie Worship Studio*

To Tom and Linda Lange, my dear friends with Life Application Ministries Publishing. Thank you so much! Couldn't have done it without you. You are awesome and Ellie loves you too!

To John Shergur ... You saw the chariots carrying the scrolls flashing through the sky – and then I saw them. They were there all along! What a sight!

To Vicki Hanson-Burkart, my fellow prayer warrior and friend …You asked the Father to open the windows of heaven for us … And He did! Thank you Lady Warrior!

To Lisa Shea, a trusted prophetic voice and seasoned soldier ... You stood on the wall for me! Because you were there – I am here!

To Chris and Angela Meadows … Thanks to my 'keepers of the script' and all things technical … We did it!

Our sincere thanks to Katie Stanley, of Katie Stanley Studio, for the author's picture on the back cover ... Katie, you are special!

To my delightful friends at 'The Rock' in Anaheim, California … Your love and ministry of Restoration is seeing thousands saved, healed and set into the ministry as you build 'solid lives.' His favor is upon you!

To my prayer partners and many friends at Elevation Church – You folks are a generation of honor walking in audacious faith while leading the way in generosity. Thanks for standing with me! You are a part of this 'Story.'

To the Lord Jesus Christ – my life was a train wreck – the vultures were after me – but you redeemed me and set me free to see others set free!

To the Holy Spirit – your still small voice and your tender touch have brought warmth and love in countless visitations and situations!

To my Father God – Abba Father – always there, always caring, always loving and always waiting for us to turn and cry out to Him!

I love you Father – Son – and Holy Spirit! Let your Name and Your Glory be magnified in all the earth.

DEDICATION PAGE

This book is first dedicated to my dear friends
Randy & Ellie Collins!
A beloved and gracious couple who are a constant reflection
and reminder of how the love of Christ truly transforms and
changes lives.
God never gave up on them and they never gave up on Father
God – their Abba Father!
They are the story of **Crossing Over!**

Also to all those to are still enslaved by a cruel task master in
the human trafficking industry – truly it is an ungodly blight
on all of humanity. Literally millions are still trapped and the
church needs to intercede that the *"God of the angel armies"*
will release His deliverance and supernatural power to set these
captives free. The job is too big for man alone, but as the Spirit
of the Lord prevailed for Ellie He can prevail for them.
Arise Church – Get in the fight – Stand in the gap
for these dear ones!

To my patient and loving wife Tonda – my Warrior Woman
– who has stood by me as I have labored through many tears
to write this *love story*. Originally this book was to be titled
"Warrior Women" and Tonda's story was also going to be told.
In a nutshell she was a part of the culture of the 'Hell's Angels
motorcycle gang', but our God also supernaturally redeemed
and restored her and now she is my "Heavenly Angel."
Her strong prophetic voice has ministered to hundreds and that
same voice has many times kept me out of the ditch!
You are an awesome 'Warrior Woman' and wife!
I love you!

Ish

A SPECIAL DEDICATION

To my sweetheart Ellie, with Love Randy!

To my own "Ms Ellie" the love of my life and most awesome wife – you have been the greatest gift my loving Father God could ever give me!

How wonderful our journey together has been over these 12 years!

As a husband I could never have a better friend and more devoted partner than you have been. What a joy to rejoice with you in both life and ministry. Loving you is absolutely the easiest thing I could ever do, as you are the most loving and sweet woman I have ever known – and you continue to radiate with beauty on both the inside and the outside.

Daily I am amazed at the people who make known to me how special you are to them. Your vibrant smile along with your warm and nurturing touch is a transforming power flowing by the love of the Lord Jesus radiating from your life!

I remember well when the Spirit of the Lord spoke to me and said *"Son you get to wake up every morning to Ellie's love and her grace. This is a woman plucked from the fire and I have joined her to you so that you would know You are home. From the first time you put you arm around her it was your heavenly father revealing His love to both of you."*

My sweet Ellie, I often ask our God "How could this woman you have blessed me with survive such a painful childhood and unspeakable abuse – and yet walk through life with the most awesome smile I have ever seen? The Father always answers the same way …. *"Because I have always loved her and I had a plan for Ms Ellie – and on her walks with me I give her new reasons to smile!"*

We are **Crossing Over** together and that my precious Ellie gives me reason to smile! I love you!

TABLE OF CONTENTS

PREFACE

What you are about to read is a true story. It is not always a pretty story, and it is not a 'reality' show. No! It is a story of life – a horrific and painful life lived by a beautiful peasant girl in Honduras. A girl who only wanted to have shoes so she could be more comfortable walking the mile to the river to carry the water for her family. Her only ambition was to go to school. Maybe, just maybe she could go to school – and grow up to become a teacher.

Those dreams were not to be. Not yet anyway. Those dreams were shattered as she never knew her father, not even his name for sure. The only men in her life were vicious predators using this little girl for their own perverted and degrading pleasures.

Total confusion about who her mother was. Was she her aunt or her mother? Why was she shuffled around from house to house? Was the woman she usually lived with really her grandmother?

Sexually abused by her stepfather and stepbrother by the age of 13. Raped by a friend's uncle at the age of 14.

Why would she be forced to marry a known sexually sadistic alcoholic pervert as she just turned 16, and he was over 30 years old?

Where are you God?

Was she sterile from her husband's sexual abuse – or was it from the three years she was forced to work in the human sex trafficking club?

Who was Adela? Was she a kind compassionate woman or just another predator parasite preying on young girls who were totally unable to defend themselves? She was a predator who, without the help of an angel would have been the total destruction of Ellie!

What were the 'vulture talons' Ellie felt in her head and in her heart?

Why did Ellie have to carry a knife everywhere she went – always within reach?

When the 'wild cat' showed up to disfigure Ellie, her friend Rubia was there to help her deflect the attack and put the demented human cat down.

But it was also heartbreaking to know that the 'wild cat' was destroyed in the process!

Cry with me as I write the story of Rubia, aka 'Lady Blanca,' and the last time Ellie saw her. Ellie had been delivered, but Rubia was dying – the once beautiful, vivacious gal had been destroyed by the life at the 'club'. You too will weep as you feel Ellie's pain at having to leave her friend!

So many others destroyed as well!

Who was Efrain? Why did he have to die? He was just a nice kid!

Wow! God showed up as she cried out to Him!

"Our Father in heaven …" Powerful words of deliverance for Ellie!

Do you believe in angels? If not you will believe as you read the thrilling testimony of Monica the bar tender, Lourdes the bus rider and Paul Grace the realtor. There is no other reasonable explanation!

Ellie has angels assigned to her and you have angels assigned to you as well. Hebrews 1:14 & Hebrews 13:2.

What was more frightening – hiding in the belly of the bus – being transported by 'coyotes' – crawling on your belly in the midst of snakes and scorpions – or crossing a river with fast moving water up to your chest? The freedom was worth it!

I am an American citizen!

Education at last! Good job – better job – great job!

How does Larry Flint fit into Ellie's picture?

Can you become 'born again' watching a TV program? Ellie was!

God 'set her up' many times as He revealed Ellie was the focus of His love!

With each having their own personal issues and challenges, how were Pastor Randy and Ellie emotionally and spiritually prepared to walk as a married couple manifesting the glory of our Lord Jesus? The answer will melt your heart and prepare your heart to walk as a Godly husband or wife!

How did Ellie get free from all the 'deep inner core pain' caused by the years of abuse and betrayal?

Can you be free?
Do you want to be free?
God wants you free as Ellie is free!
Let Ellie teach you as you read this story of the final victories!!
Are you ready to begin your own
Crossing Over?
Now is the time!!

CROSSING OVER

I'm willing to leave the familiar
I'm willing to leave what I know
If You go with me

I'm willing to go where You lead me
I'm willing to do what You say
If You stay with me

Crossing over, crossing over
Leaving all I know behind
Crossing over and not knowing what I'll find

Yes I'm crossing over, crossing over
Leaving all I know behind
Crossing over and not knowing what I'll find

But I'm crossing over, crossing over
Leaving all I know behind
Crossing over, knowing that it's You I'll find...

Song written by Kathi Wilson
Living Water Productions, LLC
www.Living-Water-Productions.com

Part 1

"CROSSING OVER"

Introduction

Dateline:
Newport Beach, California
Spring 2003

Rick & Julie Sherburne, our dear friends, had invited Tonda and me to come and share the truths of spiritual restoration with a number of home groups, as well as some congregational meetings at the Vineyard church in Laguna Niguel. It was an exciting time. We did twelve separate meetings in seven days and many personal ministry sessions as well. Many lives were changed as we taught His truth of lining up our heart and mind with the heart and mind of God which brings about transformation in body, soul and spirit.

We met Ellie and her husband Pastor Randy Collins during a morning meeting at the Sherburne home. There were close to 100 people present for the meeting, and even though their home is spacious, there were people seated everywhere; many were even seated on the stairs. The presence of the Lord was tangible as we taught on the power of His resurrected life working in our life to set us free from dis-ease and torment.

Randy and Ellie had come following a phone call from Rick the week before. Rick had told Randy "I understand you are the restoration pastor and I believe this man Ish, from North Carolina, has some truths to teach that are life transforming – please come!"

I was already speaking when Randy and Ellie arrived,

and from my position I could not really see them, but did get a glimpse of them as they walked in. My initial thought was that the glory of God was resting on this beautiful woman. She was striking; and later, after meeting her, I found her to be delightful and very gracious. There were so many people there that we did not have much time, but in another meeting I invited Randy, Ellie and other pastors and wives to help me share communion and pray for the people. I saw that the power of God and His grace were on this couple and hoped to spend more time with them.

It was almost 2 years later when Randy contacted me and asked if I could come and help him get a "Restoration" ministry jump-started. He reminded me of our first meeting and that he was intrigued when he heard this southern voice say, "IF there was a reason that you were tormented or sick, would it not be wonderful to learn what the 'IF' was?" He wanted me to come and share what the "IF" was and how to deal with it. That was 5 years ago and now Randy and Ellie have trained close to 1,000 people in ongoing classes teaching on "Resolution and Restoration."

Story of "Crossing Over"

During my ministry trips to Orange County I often stayed with Randy and Ellie, and we quickly became good friends. We frequently hiked the nature trails below their house in Anaheim Hills and had wonderful fellowship talking about the Lord. I got to know them more and more, but had never heard Ellie's story. Randy had casually mentioned that Ellie's testimony was powerful, but honestly, she was such a 'together' gal that I figured that her 'story' was probably just something like "I was lost and now I'm found." That alone is glorious, but wow, Ellie's story is much more than that. Oh yeah, much more!

It was actually another couple of years before I heard Ellie share; and as God would have it we were back in the Sherburne home doing a morning meeting with a group of Julie's friends

18

and prayer partners.

I had been praying about what to share that beautiful spring day, but all I heard the Lord speak in 'His still small voice' to me was *"Have Ellie give her testimony – these gals need to hear it!"* Wow! I didn't know about those gals, but I needed to hear it!

When she finished there was not a dry eye in the place, and you could have heard a pin drop. Frankly, we were all kind of speechless. Personally, I was stunned at her testimony. Never in a million years would I have guessed that Ellie had been through even a fraction of the things that she shared with us that morning. No! Not even a fraction!

You see, I had known Ellie for years, and obviously knew that she was a 'together woman.' No hint of emotional or spiritual damage. She was a pastor's wife – ministering to hundreds in the role of pastor herself – a business owner dealing with a number of Hollywood personalities, well known in the area.

Ellie and I had ministered many times together from the pulpit bringing broken people into the love of their Father God. We did this by working them through issues of 'forgiving' their natural father and mother for the sins the father and mother had committed against them. I remember a couple of times when Ellie would almost be overcome with emotion as she ministered to these folks that were badly bruised and broken – particularly the mother issues. So I was shocked to hear and learn of the hell and horrors that she had endured.

I knew in that moment that we had to tell Ellie's story

Ellie's story is about all of the things you pray never happen to your daughter. It is a story of poverty, neglect, abuse, betrayal, constant fear, torment and absolute hopelessness.

It reminds me of the journey that Joseph was on as a slave and prisoner in Egypt.

Joseph was used and abused, beaten, taken advantage of, betrayed, defiled, humiliated and terrorized – all by his family. Then, following his family's abuse and the betrayal of selling him as a common slave, he lived for many years as a slave in the harshest of human conditions; and with the cruelest of taskmasters.

Ellie, a beautiful peasant girl from Honduras, was also used and abused, beaten, taken advantage of, betrayed, defiled, humiliated and terrorized – all by her family. But just as Joseph was delivered, so was Ellie.

And just as Joseph was delivered to set many people free, so Ellie has been delivered and is setting many people free!

She is no longer a peasant girl, but a Mighty Warrior Woman, a daughter of the Most High God. She is now shouting His victory and His glory to many, many people and they are all being transformed by His love flowing from her and through her!

Today, Ellie is a Warrior Woman who has Crossed Over!

The story of Ellie's *Crossing Over* is not for the squeamish – the faint hearted – nor the timid! No, this story is for those longing to see the restoration, redemption and His glorious grace be showered out on desperate and lost lives. This story will give you courage. This story will provoke you to be involved in the lives of the countless people who have suffered as Ellie did. This story will make you thankful for all the blessings that you have even in bad times.

Are you ready? You will cry. You will feel her pain and understand her heartbreak. Yet, you will rejoice as you see His grace and His power and His angels set this dear one free.

CHAPTER 1

The Beginning!

It was another hot and muggy day, and the fragrance from the spring flowers were exquisite; but the insanity in the air felt oppressive to the young girl who lived in constant fear and torment.

"Why God?" Ellie cried. "Why is this happening again to me and my sister?" The problem was that she was not even sure if the God she had heard about was even real. Apparently the priests she had heard about who were supposed to know God and about God were never around to help. She often cried out to God, but He seemed to be a distant thought in her campesinos mind and she wondered if He even existed at all. She had no idea of an outside world and it would be years later before she learned that the term campesinos meant peasant. To her the torment that she lived under was 'normal' as it seemed that many of the folks she knew had similar stories or situations. The local police were deaf, blind or just totally indifferent to the cries of the campesinos!

There seemed to be no rhyme or reason to the outbursts, but here she came again with the dreaded rope and whip. There was no escape and soon the rope was around her sister's neck and she was dragging her across the rough floor while beating her with the whip. The screams were terrible and you would have thought that the neighbors would have intervened, but not in this culture. The honor of the family was paramount and most were left alone to deal with their own families as they saw fit.

She was choking, struggling for air, clawing at the rope while trying to stand up to protect herself. But it was no use. Every lash of the whip would leave a welt and often the splinters from the floor from being dragged around by the neck would later fester and leave small scars after the infection cleared up. The beating and dragging would last till the bloodletting in her grandmother's heart was done!

Later Ellie would come to know and understand that while the enemy was trying to destroy her family, her heavenly Father had a plan for her and His hand was on her, even in the horror of those moments.

It would be years later till she knew any real peace and rest, in both body and mind; as the enemy of her soul was determined to claim her for his deeds and his dark kingdom. But God, our great redeemer, through Jesus was going to set her free.

Early Life

Ellie was born into a Honduran peasant family and never owned a pair of shoes until she was over 10 years old. Of course, she didn't know they were peasants, as every family in their village was in the same boat. Honduras is one of the poorest and least developed countries in Central America, and the majority of the peasant families live in rural areas away from main roads. This adds to their burden as the people basically have to 'police' themselves because there is very little police assistance, and absolutely no government assistance for the poor.

These facts contributed to Ellie's horrendous upbringing. You are on your own and at the mercy of degenerate minds and perverted historical culture!

Survival is paramount in the peasant's mind, while education to most is only an idle and unreachable dream.

No Water and No Electricity

Ellie said, "The biggest memory of my early years was that of walking. Yes just walking. We had no water and we had to walk about an hour to the river where we would do our laundry. Then on the return trip we would carry our water for drinking. I never really thought of it as being hard. It was what all the people in La Guna our small village of about 1,000 people did. We saw buses occasionally as they passed through La Guna, and we often dreamed of the places those buses were coming from or were going to. But it was all a dream. Few ever left the villages!"

The rural society in Honduras resembles the inner city of America as most of the families have large numbers of kids; and the households are generally run by women. Over half of the families have no father and that was Ellie's plight as well. She never knew her father and thought for many years that her mother was her aunt. She was raised by her cruel grandmother till she was 11 years old when she was moved in with her mom. It was then that she was told her mom was her mom, not her aunt. Talk about confusion!

"I was so confused", said Ellie. "Yet I was excited to be with my mother, as I knew that now I would be safe and she would take care of me. Unfortunately, I didn't understand the culture and the overwhelming need for survival. The men, who were the fathers, seem to float around like 'honey bees' taking what they wanted from any of the vulnerable women who were desperate for support. Very few were actually legally married as it cost money to get married, and you had to have a priest from the Catholic Church marry you. There was no such thing as going to the courthouse and having the justice of the peace perform a legal ceremony without money."

Finally a Father

"However, my mother and stepfather were legally married and I was now going to be part of a real family. It was so exciting to be with my mom and her new husband! Now maybe my life would change and I could concentrate on school, which was so much fun. My stepfather seemed like a decent man, and best of all he had a good job at the banana company, providing for us financially. Living with my grandmother in a one room hut was now replaced by an adobe hut of three rooms. Yes three rooms! Actually, we all built the hut, which was on the plantation property, and honestly it seemed like a palace to the one room that I had moved out of. Hey, it had a tin roof! And it had running water and electricity! Unbelievable to my young mind, but true just the same."

House Slave

"Later, I realized that my stepfather was a dangerous 'honey bee'. Yet bees procreate and they had four more kids – one right after the other. Not fun for me for I was not only expected, but required to care for my four new siblings. I was nothing more than a 'house slave' and even the school I loved was slipping away due to my responsibilities. School was my refuge, but there were no laws to keep me in school, so I was subject to my mother and stepfather's demands. And their demands were that I take care of the house and kids! You've heard that saying 'barefoot and pregnant'? Well, that was my mother. I loved my siblings, but I thought when I moved in with my mom I was going to finally get some attention from her – that it was not going to happen. There was no time for me."

"I found myself growing more and more bitter toward my mother and my siblings, and would only understand years later that the 'wicked one' was playing me as I was taking on the disappointment and pain of rejection."

"A normal day for me consisted of changing diapers, washing diapers, cleaning, cooking and anything else that needed to be done. I was never just a young girl playing and studying. No! Just work! Diapers, diapers and more diapers; cleaning, cooking, cleaning again and always the diapers! My mother was often sick (constantly pregnant) so I was more of a 'work animal' than a daughter. Remember, it was about survival, and all my friends in the area were basically dealing with the same issues. Normally, if you got out of the 4th grade you would be considered lucky. Really, all your future held was, maybe – just maybe – you would end up with a husband that would actually love you, marry you and really care for you. I can only remember a couple gals in our area who were ever that fortunate."

The 'Killer Bee' comes

"Well, what was bad – got even worse," said Ellie. "Yes, much worse! Life was already hard, although hard life in this Honduran culture was normal and no one really knew the difference. There was really nothing to compare it to. Life was what it was. It was all we knew."

She hated the night. She hated the dark. Night and darkness meant one of the 'killer bees' might come. What were the 'killer bees'? Her stepfather and stepbrother were both abusers. She called them 'killer bees' because they stole your dignity and your peace by their sexual abuse and emotional terrors. They stole from her what should have been reserved for her future husband. They didn't care about her. They only cared about their own lust. To the 'bees' she was not a human being – not just an innocent young 13 year old girl – but a captured pet on a short leash.

She thought she saw the curtain tremble. She couldn't be sure. Maybe it was just someone getting up to go to the outhouse. The breeze could be coming in from the side window of the hut. She sure hoped so. The 'bees' were night creatures.

They waited till they thought the family was asleep before they 'stung'. She slept so lightly that sometimes she could sneak out before the bees came. Not tonight.

Her stepfather was suddenly there. She had only seen the curtain tremble, but now he was sitting on the bed with her. His hand was over her mouth and he was whispering in her ear terrible threats about what would happen to her and her siblings if she cried out. A real life horror story for a 13 year old. What could she do? It was too late to run. And besides, he was holding her firmly and instinctively she knew he was out of control. The bee was dangerous. Totally helpless is the only way to describe her.

No Safety Net

"Yes! Life just got worse! The defilement and fear was horrible, but what followed later was even worse. I finally got the courage to say something to my mother about what had happened, and was continuing to happen, but my plea fell on deaf ears. I went to her and showed her the blood on my clothes from the abuse, but she told me I was making it up and just having my period! My mother was my 'safety net', but my net was also full of holes. I was hung out to dry, alone and full of shame and fear. She got furious at me for even suggesting this man who was taking care of us would do such a thing. I am not sure which was worse, his defilement of my spirit and body, or my mother refusing to believe me. Looking back, I realized my Mother was in 'denial' and she knew that a confrontation would mean losing her 'banana worker killer bee.' Then, all of us would be even further on our own and out in the cold."

"In time I realized that my mother was also being physically and sexually abused by the killer bee. Because of the close confines of our three room house, you could hear a lot of what was going on. Often, I would be awakened by the pitiful muffled cries of my mother. I tried to talk to her about the 'crying' that I heard, but again she would deny everything and defend the killer bee."

"Another tragedy of the culture was that everyone was in the same boat, and the life circumstances I am describing were all to normal for most people. There were no social departments, police departments or churches that you could go to for help. You were on your own and your goal was the daily grind of survival!"

A Friend's Uncle

"I made the mistake of running away once! I was assisted by the uncle of a good friend of mine. He was so sweet and promised me that he could get me a better place to live with some really nice folks who would treat me with love and respect. He arranged to meet me about a mile from the house in an old beat up truck."

"Yikes! Suddenly I realized that I was in the presence of another 'killer bee'. This one just looked nicer and talked sweeter, but under all that veneer, he was still a dangerous predator. We had not gone far down a lonely road when he stopped and put a knife in my side and gave me the options of being left for dead or sex."

Ellie jumped from the old truck and ran for her life, believing that she could get away from her attacker. She ran through the woods too terrorized to even scream. Running and running, the tree limbs and brambles scratching and clawing at her flesh. She felt like she was running a gauntlet through a band of marauding rapists. The tearing limbs felt like the bony fingers of decaying skeletons – reaching out to grab her out of the darkness. She hated the darkness. She ran and ran, but stumbled on a root and as she fell, he pounced on her and trapped her to the ground.

"Again, I was terrified and knew that there was no one around to help me and if I resisted and got hurt badly or killed, no one even knew I was with him. I was running away and this was our big secret. He had made sure that no one knew!"

"Again, I was alone at the whims of a predator animal. I fought anyway, no longer caring – but to no avail. He still raped me and acted like I was supposed to enjoy it! Honestly, at that point I would have killed him if I could have!"

Constant Fear

"Fear was my constant companion – always knowing and always dreading the 'killer bee' was coming tonight, my stepbrother or another friend's uncle. Fear would continue to be my constant companion till many years later I found 'true peace' in the arms of my Heavenly Father!

Unfortunately, the horror of my stepfather was just the beginning of many more horrors for me with men. But it looked like a great turnaround was coming!"

A New Start!

"My escape was to 'daydream' about going to school, and maybe even becoming a teacher so I could help all the kids like me. I thought about running away, but there was nowhere to run to. I knew if I ran away there was good chance I would end up either dead, or begging for food somewhere. Even in my little community, I had heard the terrible stories about what happened to girls who fled!"

"You can imagine the excitement that coursed through me when I came home one day from the market and there on the floor of our little sitting room was my small tattered suitcase. I just knew my Mother was going to send me somewhere I could go to school. Now I was going to be out of this mess. My heart soared with love for my Mother. I had been wrong about her. She did love me and now she was sending me somewhere for a new start!"

"My elation was quickly deflated when she told me she

and 'killer bee' had arranged for me to be married to Miguel, a man from our community. Miguel had been to our little house many times, and I had always felt uneasy about him. He had a reputation for being a 'drunk' and a 'womanizer'. She told me that there was no money to take care of me and the four new kids, therefore, this was being arranged for everyone's benefit. I realized later my mother and 'killer bee' had been told by one of my sister's friends who had tried to seduce me I was nothing but a common whore and would only cause them trouble, as well as money. The boy was a real creep and he had chased me all through the woods tearing at my clothes and trying to rape me! Since he was unsuccessful – other than terrorizing me – he lied to my mother. She believed him. I learned at an early age that men were deceitful and not to be trusted. Not trusting men was another lie of the enemy to keep me in bondage for many years."

"But I don't want to get married, I remember screaming! And certainly not to this man who was a known alcoholic and a sexual creep! Not to mention that I was barely 16 and had just finished the 6th grade and Miguel was over 30 years old."

"Sadly, in the Honduran culture, I was trapped, and had no choice but to leave with him when he came for me. I tried to be tough and was hopeful that this marriage would be all right and bearable. In my young mind I said 'well maybe this will really work out and he will really love me and care for me as a woman.' I quickly found out that the hellish life I had been living was only going to get worse. And I do mean worse!"

Another Killer Bee

"I was forced to go to the local authorities and sign some papers saying I had agreed with the arrangement, which of course I didn't. It was then I realized my life was going to get worse, not better. Standing in the official building with my mother, her 'killer bee' and my soon to be husband, who was looking at me with looks that only later I understood to be totally lecherous! I remember thinking 'I am only a young girl and never been intimate with a man voluntarily and now I am being forced to marry!"

"I realized many years later that the pain and betrayal of knowing my mother was allowing this to happen to me was worse than the pain and agony of the physical and sexual abuse that I suffered at the whim of this sadist. I was totally alone and there was no one – absolutely no one – who cared whether I lived or died. That abandonment alone was complete horror for a 16 year old peasant girl! Years later I learned the words of Jesus and felt they applied to me – *"My God, Why has thou forsaken me?"* I truly felt forsaken and totally alone. Yes, totally alone!"

"The beatings started immediately and never stopped until I escaped months later. His perverted sexual appetite knew no bounds; and when I did not consent to his demands immediately, I was physically beaten and repeatedly sexually abused. Again, there was no one nor any organization that I could run to for help. Basically, I was his property to do with as he pleased. Much of the time I stayed tied to the wall in the bedroom so that I would be available for his sadistic and perverted desires. It was not till years later that I realized I was sterile, and my inability to be able to conceive was due to injuries inflicted on me from this sadistic man."

Cousin Besy found me!

Six months later Besy, Ellie's dear friend and cousin came looking for her. No one had seen her, or heard from Ellie since her arranged marriage, and Besy wanted to have 'girl talk' and catch up on things.

It was a divine appointment that Besy came when she did, as Miguel's sadistic nature was becoming more and more violent with each passing week.

When Besy found the hut she knocked on the door, but

no one answered. She was able to look in through the cracks in the door and what she saw made her go weak in the knees. Ellie said, "She saw me tied to the wall with my hands over my head. My clothes were half torn off of leaving me exposed and I was bleeding and bruised from the most recent beating and abuse."

Besy really freaked out as she was expecting to find Ellie a happy little wife just getting on with life. But what she found was a beaten and abused 16 year old girl – her very cousin – whom she loved dearly!

Unfortunately, in Honduras and many other similar nations, the police will not, or can't help you. The culture is one of misogamy (hatred of women) and it has been that way for generations, even thousands of years.

So what did you do?

"So what did you do," I asked Ellie? "We ran for our lives! Fortunately Besy had some money with her and we ran till we could catch a bus to get us as far away as possible. We didn't care where it went – just away from the violent Miguel and his reach. We knew we had to be a long way away, and we ended up in San Pedro which was a much larger city of about 100,000 people. It was a long way from the village and hopefully safe. We knew no one and no one knew us!"

Finally some kindness

After arriving in San Pedro, they got off the bus and continued walking toward the town. Neither of them had seen a town this big, much less a city. There were people everywhere – all kinds of hustle and bustle – which they found exciting. They were just two peasant girls coming to town for the first time in their lives. Totally naïve were these gals and truly at the mercy of others. They kept walking and gawking at all the sights around them and then they came upon a large restaurant.

There was a woman standing out front who looked to be more of Indian descent as opposed to Hispanic and she spoke kindly to Ellie and Besy. She introduced herself as Adela and told them she was the owner of the restaurant and club.

Adela asked Ellie, "How did you get so beat up?" "I told her the story and she seemed to be very sympathetic and took me to the doctor and then to a clothing store. She also bought me many nice things like make up which I had never really had before. I was thrilled when she said I could work for her in the restaurant and pay her back over time with wages." Besy was also thrilled. Finally Ellie was in a safe place. She sure deserved it after all she had been through with Miguel and his torture.

Ellie recalled later she and dear Besy talked about how different it was here in the city! People were really nice to them. They seemed to care about you. No one had ever taken the time to take Ellie to the doctor. Certainly no one had ever bought her those expensive things like lipstick, eye shadow, hosiery, even fancy undergarments! Wow, the girls really laughed about those things. In fact, Adela tried to buy things for Besy and talk her into staying. But Besy had her own responsibilities to her family and she left with a promise not to say a word about where Ellie was. In Besy's mind Ellie could not have been in a better place than with this restaurant owner Adela. To both girls Adela was one of the nicest and kindest people they had ever met.

Health Returns

Days turned into weeks and Ellie's health was starting to return. Ellie said "This was actually a peaceful time as I worked for Adela in the restaurant. Adela made sure I was eating regularly and took me to the doctor a few more times. That was different as I had never had a physical before. She taught me how to apply make up and fix my hair, providing me with expensive shampoos and conditioners. The meals were simple, but they were regular. In the village we had only eaten corn, rice, beans and cheese. In Adela's house I still ate a lot of corn, rice, beans and cheese, but there also was mixed in a lot of protein, such as eggs and chicken. Along with the better diet, she made me take vitamins. She placed me in a private room near her own living quarters and checked on me regularly. Honestly, she treated me more like a daughter than a peasant girl who had come in all beat up and desperate. Life was good and I felt it was only going to get better."

"Years later I would look back on Adela's kindness and realize she was actually preparing me to 'pay her back' for her kindness. I was a meal ticket for her – I just didn't know it at the time. I never thought it would be what it was – a new living hell!"

"It was the price of the **'payback'** that was going to further trap me and almost destroy me – just a simple peasant girl trying to survive!"

*"So when the Midianite merchants
came by, his brothers pulled Joseph
up out of the cistern and <u>sold him</u> for
twenty shekels of silver to the
Ishmaelities who took
him to Egypt."*

Genesis 37:28 (NIV)

*"Meanwhile the Midianites
<u>sold Joseph</u> in Egypt to Potiphar, one
of Pharaoh's
officials, the captain of the guard."*

Genesis 37:36 (NIV)

CHAPTER 2

Adela's Payback – another hell!

Life to an uneducated peasant girl new to the big city can be an exciting time. To say Ellie was 'naïve' would be very true. She was not naïve to the ways of the peasant culture and the little villages – she had already seen and experienced the darkness with her step dad, her step brother, her predacious husband as well as the friend's uncle who raped her and terrorized her. Ellie, in all her 16 years, had never known any real joy. She had friends in the village and the most peaceful time they had was the long walks to the river. Even those river walks could be scary as it seemed like every male in the society was either trying to seduce you or abuse you. It was true of all of the girls, but especially true of the pretty ones. That made Ellie an even bigger conquest target as she was definitely one of the prettiest. Of course, Ellie had her cousin Besy, and they stood up for each other and protected each other. If you started trouble with Ellie or Besy – you better be prepared to fight the other one as well.

It was only a matter of days before Besy felt like Ellie was in good hands and with another promise to not reveal her location she headed for home. Ellie just kept working hard for Adela and enjoyed being pampered for a season.

Patio Confrontation

Ellie had noticed that a number of girls seemed to always be hanging around in the afternoon out by the patio. The patio was located in the back of the building in a nice area surrounded by flowers and bordered by a small, but swift flowing stream. Ellie loved to go there in the afternoon hours when she was off and just enjoy the quietness and the calmness. Quietness and calmness were two things this young peasant girl had little experience with.

It was during one of those quiet peaceful afternoons sitting by the stream that Ellie started realizing that things were not as she had thought. The quiet was broken by a large boned girl who looked more like a man that a woman. She reminded Ellie of a wild tabby cat, all snarl and bristle. She came up to Ellie's chair with a couple other girls and demanded to know who she was and what was she doing there. Ellie replied, "I am a friend of Adela's and I am working for her in the restaurant." Ellie felt safe, confident that Adela was her friend and would take care of her. After all, had not Adela fed her, clothed her, taken her to the doctor and given her meaningful work and a place to live? Ellie's reply seemed to incense the tabby cat girl and Ellie thought for sure she heard this scary looking gal growl at her.

The girl then reached down and dragged Ellie out of the chair and told her not to mess with any of her men. "I am Marcela and you don't mess with me – nobody messes with me and my men." She then stormed off with the girls leaving Ellie standing there wondering what just happened. Wow! This is too weird. Ellie went to find Adela to find out who these girls were.

A Real Shock!

Ellie was still shaking from the confrontation when she found Adela in the restaurant kitchen. When Adela saw Ellie come in, she went to her and Ellie told her what happened. Adela replied, "Yes, I know Marcela. In fact, she works for me in the club. Her job is to entertain men in the club and she is what is known as a courtesan. Actually, she came to me very much in the same way you came to me Ellie. She was abused by her father and uncle and after running away to escape their constant abuse, she found herself on the streets and had to turn tricks to eat. I found her and took her in. Now she is paying me back for all the money she owes me while hoping to meet a nice man who will take her to be his wife."

Ellie was mystified. "How come I have never seen her? I have been here with you for almost two months and she has never been around. I have been in the restaurant every day working for you and have seen some girls all dressed up come in together, but I never saw this Marcela. She was mean and was really ugly to me. And what is this club? And who are these men she told me not to mess with? Is it the other building that kind of joins the restaurant on the other side?

"Slow down Ellie and let me explain," said Adela. "You have never seen her because she works in the men's club which is on the other side of the restaurant. The other girls are friends of Marcela's and they also work for me in the men's club as entertaining courtesans."

"What do you mean a courtesan? What is a courtesan? I never heard of such a job. And what is this club?" "Actually" Adela said, "a courtesan is a very common occupation for girls in our society. We find it to be very honorable and it is a quick way to get out of your debt. You know Ellie you owe me a lot of money for the food, make up, clothes, physicians. There is also, of course, rent on the nice room over my restaurant." And after a moment Adela added, "Ellie, you owe me a lot of money for all I have done for you. I expect for you to pay me back. To pay me back you will join Marcela as another one of the girls. Currently, we have eleven girls in residence that work the club as entertainers or courtesans." Ellie was appalled when Adela explained what a courtesan was and what she expected Ellie to do as an entertainer in the club. Adela told her "Mainly you just get the men to buy more champagne and liquor. Just dance with them, be nice to them and make them feel at home. For most of them that is all they want anyway. Ellie you are a gorgeous girl and that is why Marcela was upset with you. She sees you as a threat even though you are not actually working in the club yet."

Ellie was stunned! She was having trouble getting her breath. The reality of Adela's words sank in revealing that she was again trapped with no escape. There were no police she could run to who would listen. There were no organizations to go to for help. She was trapped, trapped, trapped! Again trapped! She was captured in another cage just like she had been with her grandmother, her mother, her step dad, her step brother, and her friend's uncle. Again, she had been betrayed, used, manipulated, and had become the victim of a new kind of 'predator'. A predator who had disguised herself as a mothering, caring person – Adela's betrayal pain was maybe the hardest. She was now Adela's prisoner and the only way out was the **'payback'**. And the payback was going to be a new breed of hell!

The fear at the moment caused her blood to leave her head, her knees weakened and her body shook almost uncontrollably. She sat there at the table with Adela and wept, not believing what she was hearing. Trapped == trapped == trapped!

Adela called the bartender over and for the first time in her life Ellie had an alcoholic drink. Adela said it was medicinal and would make her feel better. She almost screamed at Adela "I don't want to feel better, I want to be free. I am 16 years old and I am not your slave, or anybody's slave – not now and not ever!" Adela coaxed her into the drink and it did make her feel better, but it also became a crutch and another trap!

Decisions and Choices

Ellie sat there in the restaurant with Adela and had another drink. It really didn't taste bad and she was starting to feel less concerned about her situation. Adela told her, "Ellie, go on to bed and think about your decision. Are you going to pay me back working in the club, or do I have to turn you over to the police as a fraud?"

The next morning Ellie was up before daylight just walking around the streets and trying to figure out what to do. Basically, she knew that she only had a few choices. One choice would be to return to her peasant village and her sadistic husband Miguel. That was not going to happen. She knew he would probably kill her if not worse! According to the law she was legally married to Miguel, even if the marriage was arranged and forced. The so-called government authorities would have forced her to live with him again.

She could just run away, but where would she run? There was nowhere to go. She had already seen the tragic results of the peasant girls who ran away from the village. Some had actually ended up here in San Pedro and had been enslaved by pimps who cared about nothing but the next fistful of money. Some had been kidnapped off the streets and were sold as sex slaves never to be seen again. Girls who end up in the sex slave trade are never heard from again – baring a divine miracle. It is a well established fact that most prostitution and sex slavery is the direct result of desperate poverty. Parents and other adults regularly sell their children to visiting tourists. This has now been labeled *'sex tourism'*. The amount of money being made is staggering. It is estimated that more than 50 billion dollars per year is generated through this evil practice.

Most authorities designate the sex slave trade and other components of it as human trafficking. A good definition of human trafficking is: ***"the practice of people being tricked, lured, coerced or otherwise removed from their home or country, and then forced to work with low or no payment or on terms which are highly exploitative. The practice is considered to be the trade or commerce of people, which has many features of slavery, and which is illegal in most countries. The victims of human trafficking are used in a variety of situations, including prostitution, forced labor (including bonded labor or debt bondage) and other forms of involuntary servitude."***

Sex trafficking is defined by the US State Department as ***"when a person is coerced, forced or deceived into prostitution, or maintained in prostitution through coercion."***

While researching the sex slave trade I came across a quote illustrating the depravity and disgusting nature of this multibillion dollar business. Quoting from U.S Department of Justice, Child Exploitation and Obscenity Section was a Retired U. S. Schoolteacher:

"On this trip I've had sex with a 14 year old girl in Mexico and a 15 year old in Columbia. I'm helping them financially. If they don't have sex with me, they may not have enough food. If someone has a problem with me doing this, let UNICEF feed them."

Another testimony from the same web site was:

"Maria is ... prostituted by her aunt. Maria is obliged to sell her body exclusively to foreign tourists in Costa Rica; she only works mornings as she has to attend school in the afternoon. Maria is in the fifth grade."

Ellie was just as forced to work as a courtesan for Adela as these kids were forced to work for an aunt or retired school teacher in Costa Rica and Mexico. All of these folks are what I see as victims of a sin-cursed world! This was not something they chose, but something that they were forced or manipulated to participate in.

Could she go to the police? No. They would either force her to go back to her husband, or even worse, with the corruption she could become enslaved in an even worse place. No, the police were not going to help her, and she saw that vividly a couple years later with her friend Efrain, who only wanted to be her protector, but it cost him his life.

Some ask "How about a missionary society or the church?" If the societies were there, none of the girls had ever heard of them. The church was also basically non-existent as far as the girls were concerned.

What about her mother? Could she go there? No! Her mother had never understood what was going on. She was a victim herself and could not be counted on to protect her.

"I am going to destroy you!"

Ellie remembered coming to a beautiful stream near the edge of town where there were some benches. There seemed to be a measure of peace as the water was swift where the stream narrowed. It splashed noisily in crystalline fans over the rocks and was swirling in deep green pools. It truly was a beautiful, peaceful sight. She could almost sense something that seemed somehow holy. Something that was not natural – certainly not in this crazy situation. A temporary peace and calmness settled over her as she saw herself in America – a country she had heard about. A country full of peace and opportunity – maybe someday – but today is about survival. "What should I do," she cried!

That peace was short lived as the reality of her situation came upon her like a dark cloud. The stream was no longer pretty and peaceful. Her skin started to crawl and she felt like a hoard of vultures had landed on her and was tearing parts of her flesh off her bones. They were slowly killing her. One of the vultures had his talons embedded in her heart and another had his talons embedded in her head. They had her pinned to the ground. She was totally helpless. It was really frightening as an overwhelming evil presence seemed to speak to her saying *"you are mine – you belong to me and I am going to destroy you just as these vultures are destroying you."* Ellie would realize later that the 'wicked one' was indeed trying to kill her and his plan for her life was just that – to kill her and others as well. During her life and for the next years the enemy would tear at her spirit, her soul, and her body. Her spirit was already broken – her soul was already bitter, rejected and full of betrayal – and her body would suffer much more abuse before the Captain of her salvation would set her free. But indeed – He would set her free!

The Lesser Evil Decision

Oh, how she hated it, but she felt like she had no other

choice but to go along with Adela's plan of working the debt off in the club. It was not a good choice, but it was a choice of what she hoped was the lesser evil. And she was going to make quick work of paying back the debt. Of course, she had no idea how Adela was calculating her debt and it was much later before she knew Adela was manipulating the debt from every angle. Adela didn't want any of her girls to leave. Her girls were her bread and butter. Ellie was determined to entertain, but she was not going to be a courtesan and have sex with these men. Just get them to drink more liquor, dance with them and spend more money. Yes that would make Adela happy and she could get her debt paid. Adela was thrilled at her decision, and Ellie started that very night. She also moved her into a new room near the other girls in the club. It was best described as a motel. Again, Adela took Ellie and they bought more things for her room. Furniture and all the accessories to make the room like Ellie wanted it. Adela was really racking up Ellie's payback debt and Ellie didn't even know it! Ellie was not yet 'street smart', but she would be soon. Her 'street smarts' would keep her alive.

"The Club"

Adela helped Ellie get all dressed up in her new clothes she had bought for her, and took her to the club. There she was introduced all around and told to work with a blond headed gal named Rubia Peligrosa. Ellie and Rubia became instant friends. Their histories were similar and they were both very pretty. Rubia was this striking blond and Ellie was the gorgeous 16 year old fresh, naïve gal. Lecherous men just love fresh young gals and Ellie fit the bill. Latino men also love blonds and Rubia was a blond. It is not a bad thing to be the prettiest, but it is dangerous when you are the prettiest two gals out of the 12 that worked there.

Remember Marcela? Well she just glared at Ellie from across the room. The tension increased when an Englishman asked Ellie to dance after having danced with Marcela. That was a sure recipe for trouble in a brothel as the girls are insanely jealous for their customers. Ellie knew Marcela was dangerous and she kept a close eye on her.

Ellie made it through the first couple of nights just dancing with the men and dodging their sexual advances. Adela seemed pleased. Rubia and Ellie had made an unspoken covenant to watch after each other and Ellie felt like Rubia had replaced her cousin Besy as her protector. It was comforting to have a friend.

Ellie will never know for sure what happened, but on the third night she ended up in her new room with an Englishman who paid her handsomely for her services. More than likely she was given a date rape drug to loosen her up and squelch any resistance. Adela was probably the one who gave Ellie the drug! The drug left her with a mild headache the next morning, but then Rubia gave her some 'white powder' and showed her how to use it. After that she not only felt better, but she felt like she could take on the whole world. The white powder put her on top of the world – at least for a time.

Rubia sat with Ellie and said, "Girl, the only way to ever get out of here is to quit being Miss Prudish and do what is necessary to please these men. Adela expects it and it is the only way out of this trap. I know you hate it. I hate it too, but it is what it is and it is a fact of our lives right now. Don't fight it." Ellie replied, "Rubia that is not who I am. I just want to make them drink more liquor and spend more money – not have sex with them. Being intimate with these creeps is disgusting." "Well," Rubia replied. "How disgusting is it going to be if Adela turns you over to the police and you end up in one of their brothels? Talk about disgusting. Now that would be disgusting! Set your heart and mind on getting out of here and do what is necessary till then. I will stick with you and we will do this together – we will make it to America."

Ellie did not like any of this, but she knew she was trapped and would just have to make the best of a bad situation. At least she had Rubia. They could stick together, encourage each other, and defend each other. And to think, they were only 16 years old!

Rubia was an interesting blond. It was actually a wig. Ellie didn't even know it for quite a while as the wig looked so natural and fit so well. One slow night, as they were talking, Rubia shared with her that the 'blond' was a wig and the reason she wore it was because it came down over her 'bad' eye. It sloped from her forehead down over one eye, giving her what some would call a sexy, sultry look. Well actually, the sexy look was used to cover a bad eye. Ellie never knew for sure what happened to Rubia's eye. She had been abused as a child, often beaten and neglected, so it could have been from an injury that was never treated. There was not even an eyeball there – just an area totally covered over with scar tissue. So she wore her hair with lots of hair spray to cover the bad eye. Because of Rubia's very blond wig Ellie nicknamed her 'Lady Blanca', which means white. The name stuck and the clients as well as the girls called her 'Lady Blanca.'

Later, as Ellie was gaining her 'freedom,' Lady Blanca would be close to death and it was heart wrenching for Ellie to have to leave her friend knowing she was dying. The club had killed her. But such was life where violence, sickness and sin so ruled!

These words of Joseph could have been Ellie's words as well!

"They bruised his feet with shackles
his neck was put in irons,
and his soul entered into the iron."

Psalm 105:18 (NIV & AMP)

"I was kidnapped from the land. And since I have been here I have done nothing to deserve being put in this hole."

Genesis 40:15 (MSG)

CHAPTER 3

Life in the Brothel

During a meeting Ellie and I attended together to share her story one of the folks asked her to describe the club where she had been enslaved. Ellie replied without any hesitation. "It was hell! You can't sugar coat it. It was a living hell 24/7. Tormenting nights followed by tormenting days – but always hell. Day after day, week after week, month after month – the same torment. You cannot paint it with a sweet soft brush and make it a pretty picture. It is just ugly. There was never any peace – always lurking fear."

Fear abounding on every side.
Fear of all people. Even the ones you think are your friends.
Fear of sexual abuse.
Fear of beatings.
Fear of disease.
Fear of pregnancy.
Fear of disfigurement.
Fear of abortion.
Fear of forced or botched abortion.
Fear of Adela and her enforcement.
Fear of the police.
Fear that you will always just be an object.
Fear of being sold to another 'club.'
Fear of betrayal is your walking companion.
Fear that one of the jealous girls would ambush me.
Fear that Adela would increase my quota of men above the normal 8 to 10 per night that was expected of each girl.

"Defilement fills your nostrils with a foul cancerous stench. Washing and bathing never makes you feel clean. So you wash again, but still no feeling of being clean. I often wanted to bathe in bleach hoping that it would remove the stench of many men."

"It was many years later that I would finally be washed by the precious Lord Jesus – finally a true man – the son of God, who loved me, and gave His life for me. King Jesus, my spiritual husband, was the first man who loved me unconditonally, honored me and removed all the stench, shame and guilt from years of abuse. My dear husband, Randy was the second, and he too is a treasure."

"People sometimes ask me, 'what did the brothel or the club look like?' Well, it was not what you would call fancy by Hollywood movie standards, but it was nice and considered rather fancy in Honduras. Have you have ever seen the saloons in western movies? That is what it reminds me of," Ellie said. "The girls were all dressed up to look fancy and pretty. The cowboys were all trying to get the girls attention. Everyone was drinking and often doing drugs – it often makes for a really bad scene. Every day presented new danger and treacherous situations to navigate. Was this client going to be a murderer, an abuser, diseased, or disfigure me? Disfigurement was one of the main concerns. Girls were regularly cut if they did not live up to expectations." Ellie continued, "Adela had her bouncers and enforcement system set up to deal with the clients and they were mostly hospitable and behaved. But drunks and fools rarely behave for very long. When one of the clients really got out of hand, we never saw them again. The girls were Adela's bread winners; so she did everything necessary and possible to keep them safe. We heard stories about what happened to the bad ones, but you could never tell truth from fiction. Rumors are always a big part of the drama in such a place."

The 'Wild Cat' Strikes

The club was in full swing about 2:00 am. The girls were all over the place entertaining the clients. Tonight there were many clients from out of town and some foreigners as well. The girls liked the foreign travelers the best. They usually had the most money, and they would spend it. Some were on big company expense accounts and would really throw the money around. They saw themselves as real big shots, and liked to brag to the girls. On the other hand, they could also be the most dangerous, so you really had to be careful. This is where the 'street smarts' came into play. Some might call it intuition. Some might call it discernment. Some would call it just a woman's special sense. Regardless the girls knew to be on their toes with the foreign visitors. The music was loud, the booze was flowing and marijuana smoke hung thickly in the moist air.

Suddenly, Marcela came running in growling like a mad woman. The wild tabby cat was running loose again. She ran from girl to girl slapping each one as she ran by. Ellie saw her coming and ducked behind her date, but Marcela still was able to throw a drink on Ellie. It was obvious Ellie was the reason for her rage, and if the bouncer had not come in and grabbed Marcela, she would have slapped her also. Of course, getting slapped is no fun, but it is much better than getting cut, and Marcela had already cut a couple of the girls on the arms or back. Not the face. The face was the important thing. Adela would not put up with someone cutting her merchandise, either the paying clients or the girls. The earlier cuts were minor, only requiring a couple stitches, so Adela had let her stay – at least for a season. The season would end tonight!

Everyone thought it was all over when Marcela came back in and sat at the bar quietly drinking. The smoggy craziness returned to normal. But it was not over. It was just getting started. The 'wild cat' was looking for blood. It was Ellie's blood and pretty face that she wanted. Marcela's rage was caused by her intense jealousy of all the girls, but it was particularly focused particularly at Ellie and Rubia. After all, they were the prettiest and the most popular at the club. In Marcela's demented mind, Ellie and Rubia were the reason for all her problems.

Ellie's street smarts kicked in and she was on high alert. Her adrenaline was flowing – her muscles tense. It was no secret that one of Marcela's clients had given her an Italian switchblade stiletto knife. She carried it with her all the time and it was razor sharp. A killer knife for sure. Ellie made sure that she could see Marcela from anywhere in the club and determined to not put her back to her, or get close to where she was sitting at the bar. She was dancing with the same client from earlier, when she suddenly realized that her back was to Marcela. Just as she realized her back was turned, she saw Marcela reflected in the mirror. The wild, crazy Marcela jumped off the stool and ran towards her. Her blade flashed as the cold steel sprung from the knife glistening in the bar lights like a cobra strike. Everyone in the club froze when they saw the knife. People started running. Others were shouting. It was a chaotic scene.

Rubia saw what was happening and tried to block Marcela, but the 'wild cat' threw Rubia out of the way, slashing her on the arm in the process. Rubia's block saved Ellie, throwing Marcela off balance as she lurched at Ellie trying to cut her face. But she missed. As she went by, Ellie reacted instinctively, hitting her behind the ear with her closed fist as hard as she could. She did it without thinking. She was not aiming. She just swung. She was just trying to protect herself. The blow put the wild cat reeling and as she was going down she hit her head on the edge of the table. Marcela was out cold! She was down for the long count and then some. Fight over!

Adela, the madam, was in the corner of the bar with one of her enforcers and saw the whole thing. She jumped up and told her companion enforcer "Get her sold. She is too dangerous for my club. And get her sold tonight. I don't ever want to see her again." The bouncers picked her up, carried her out, and she was never seen again.

Girls Sold

All the girls knew girls were sold from one club to another, but this was the first time they had confirmation. They knew it was true when they heard Adela yell, "Get her sold." And it happened. They never saw Marcela again. They never knew where she went or who she went with. They only knew that she was gone. No one was upset about it as she was so dangerous and contentious. Some of the girls had actually come from other clubs located in other cities, but the details were always sketchy at best. It was difficult to have any real relationships with the girls as they were always working, or resting up from work, or resting to go back to work. It was work, work, and more work! It was not an environment that stimulated any real friendships.

Ellie and Rubia were the exception and they did become fast friends. It was their friendship that saved Ellie from the wild cat. If Rubia had not thrown her off balance, Ellie would have been badly disfigured or even killed.

Sadly, the girls didn't really understand what was happening. Remember they were all peasant girls and had no one other than the 'madam' to protect them. If that happened in America a girl could run to the nearest policeman and get help. But not in Honduras! The police were in cahoots with the brothels and they were being paid by the madam either with money or favors. The girls had no choice and no chance!

Ellie & Rubia Run Away

This was their second try. They only got a few blocks away the first time when Adela happened to come by in her car. They thought they fooled her when they told her they were just out for a walk. Maybe, maybe not; but Adela took them back to the club and nothing more was mentioned about it. They hoped it was 'case closed.'

More months went by and Ellie knew she had to try again.

She felt like she was coming apart at the seams. The long days and the longer nights were slowly killing her. It looked like she would never get Adela paid off. And paying her off was the only deliverance possible. She and Rubia decided to try and make a run for it. What could they lose? They had to try again. Surely someone would help them and they could be free to try and go to America.

They planned to leave in the early morning before dawn. They figured they could find a bus and just ride till they were far enough away to be safe. That had worked when Ellie had escaped from Miguel. It seemed like a good plan, but it didn't work. They got about a mile from the club when they were spotted by a policeman who frequented the club. He might not have noticed them, but they were each carrying a small suitcase that drew his attention. It was not unusual for people to be walking around at all hours. But it was unusual for two 17 year old girls to be walking around with a suitcase.

They knew they were in trouble when he called them by name. "Ellie and Rubia, what are you girls doing walking the streets like common streetwalkers? You should be at the club, and at this hour you should be resting." They knew they were busted. He put them in the police car and they thought he would take them back to the club. Wrong! He took them to jail and charged them with prostitution. The girls later figured out he had called Adela and told her where they were. She must have told him to keep us to teach us a lesson about running away.

The jail was a pure rat infested hellhole. There were even big roach looking bugs crawling all around the cell. This cell only had women and they were a pitiful bunch. Some of the women even had bugs crawling on them, and they didn't seem to notice. When we asked about the toilet, we were told, "It is that hole in the floor!" It literally was a hole in the floor near the wall. No toilet seat. Nothing – just a hole in the floor. Really nasty. You were just supposed to squat and do your 'business,' and the 'business' was everywhere. Worse than the hole in the floor was the pipe coming from the wall about 18 inches from the floor and very close to the toilet hole. The pipe was your only source of water in the cell. If someone was using the hole in the floor there was not room to get to the water pipe. Rubia and Ellie spent the rest of the night and most of the day in that same cell, and never used the hole or the water pipe. "It was a picture out of a horror book and we were terrified," said Ellie.

When we were finally released to Adela's custody, the police captain told us "If you end up here again trying to run away, we will put you in the cell with the men, and we have no control over what they will do to you. But we know they would love to have you teenage girls in their cell." Just the look on his face when he said that would freeze your blood. Following that experience we knew for sure that Adela was deeply connected with the police.

Joseph

Years later – having been born again = Ellie had vivid recollections of their jail cell time when she studied the lives of Joseph and Paul, as well as other Saints imprisoned for their faith in the Lord Jesus.

You see Joseph, like Ellie, was in a slave prison that his family was responsible for. Joseph's brothers sold him into slavery, just as Ellie's family arranged for her to be married – the same as being sold – since she had no choice in the matter. They were forced, manipulated and coerced – not their own decision. Joseph was in Potiphar's prison for about three years and Ellie was in Adela's prison club for three years.

*"Now we are paying for what we did to our brother – we saw
how terrified he was when he was begging us for mercy. We
wouldn't listen to him, and now we are in trouble"*
Genesis 42:21 (The Message)

*"But he sent a man on ahead:
Joseph, sold as a slave.
They put cruel chains on his ankles,
An iron collar around his neck."*
Psalms 105:17-18 (The Message)

Ellie took comfort in knowing her heavenly Father used
every horrible experience to bring honor and glory to His
name. She saw Joseph was imprisoned – not for his crimes –
but because he was a victim of cruel people. Yet, our Father
God had a plan and used Joseph mightily in that hour. Now
Ellie today, as Joseph of old, is in the ministry of setting people
free from their own prisons! Neither Joseph nor Ellie could see
in their horrible hour what God was doing in their lives to bring
deliverance to multitudes. Later, the reality of God's love was
manifest in both Joseph and Ellie!

My Friend Efrain

"It was sometime during my second year at the club when
Efrain came in," Ellie said. "He was a nice and gentle young
man and I quickly realized that he had a crush on me. While I
was flattered, I knew that I was a captive to Adela and the only
way to get free was to pay her debt."

Efrain was so taken with Ellie he would come and spend
his whole pay check just to stay with her and protect her. He
wanted nothing else from her other than to spend time with
her and keep her away from all the other men. It worked for a
while, but there must have been a lot of complaints as Adela
told Ellie she could not spend all her time with Efrain, even if
he was paying so much. They got in a heated discussion and
Ellie was screaming at Adela "What difference does it make

who pays? You still get the money!" Adela yelled right back at her something like "This is my club and you belong to me and what I say goes – and that is all there is to it!"

A few days later the police showed up at the club and wanted to see Ellie. They asked her all kinds of questions about Efrain such as, "How long have you known him? Were you planning to run away with him? Were you selling drugs for him? Do you know who he works for? Where did he get all his money?" Finally, Ellie said "I don't know the answer to any of those questions, just ask Efrain."

The police captain quietly replied. "We would ask him, but we found him dead on the road near the club. He has been murdered – shot in the head at close range."

Ellie felt like her sister must have when her grandmother dragged her around the room with a rope tightly around her neck. She could not breathe. She couldn't talk. She was choking. She wanted to sit down, but her legs wouldn't work. Adela helped her to a seat and after a few minutes, Ellie also told them about the man from last night.

Ellie told Adela and the police about the man coming into the club the night before looking for a certain girl. Could he be connected to Efrain's murder? The man walked around looking at many girls and when he got to Ellie, he put a gun to her head and said. "You are a dead woman!" Then, just as quickly, he said, "Oh I'm sorry, I grabbed the wrong girl," and fled from the club. It had really shaken Ellie as she saw in the man's eyes that he was about to kill her. No doubt he was crazy! Could he have murdered Efrain? Ellie would never know.

That night, a paralyzing fear and sadness came over. She knew in that moment – one way or another – she was going to get out of the club and be free!

*"Our Father in heaven
Hallowed be your name,
Your kingdom come,
Your will be done
on earth as it is in heaven.
Give us today our daily bread.
Forgive us our debts,
as we also have forgiven our
debtors.
And lead us not into
temptation,
but deliver us from the evil one."*

**"The Lord's Prayer"
Matthew 6:9-13 (NIV)**

CHAPTER 4

"Our Father in heaven ..."

That night of paralyzing fear and sadness was one of the most important nights of Ellie's life. As she got back to her room a nervous wreck, the walls seem to close in on her. She still could barely breathe and the vultures were circling!

So much sadness and fear during her time at the club. Many of the girls had suffered from repeated and botched abortions. A few had died from the botched abortions as the abortionists were not really doctors, just butchers. Adela would not allow the girls to keep a baby, so it was sadness on top of tragedy. Many were sick with one disease or another. Some became so strung out on drugs that they could hardly function. We were told they had been sold to another location, but we were never sure. We all hoped that was all that had happened when they disappeared in the middle of the night. No one really knew.

"I lay on my bed trying to figure out what to do – how could I get out of this prison – when suddenly I realized that I was on my knees at the side of the bed!"

"God if you are real get me out of here! Then, as my grandmother had taught us to pray I began praying … **Our Father in heaven** … But I could not remember any more of the words, so I just kept praying that one phrase … **Our Father in heaven ...** over and over, till I fell asleep."

Remember the cruel grandmother? The one that would lose control and drag Ellie's sister around by the neck while beating her? Well that same grandmother had taught the girls how to pray *The Lord's Prayer*. Deep in the heart of that grandmother there was a revelation that Jesus was the son of God. She had tried to teach the girls in her limited fashion that He was the Deliverer. Ellie had never been to a church. She had never been to a Sunday school. No one had ever read the bible to her.

She didn't even go to school till she was ten years old. Ellie would not have known Adam from Noah – Saul from Sampson – Jonah from Abraham – King David from John the Baptist – Rahab from Sarah, or our Lord Jesus from Job! In other words, at that point in her life she was totally biblically illiterate! If she had ever heard the name of Jesus, it was a distant memory and totally irrelevant.

But she called out on the name of the Lord and cried **"God if you are real, get me out of here!"** and then she followed up with **"Our Father in heaven …..."**

> *The cords of death entangled me,*
> *The anguish of the grave came upon me;*
> *I was overcome by trouble and sorrow.*
> *Then I called on the name of the LORD:*
> *"O LORD, save me!*
> **Psalm 116:3-4 (NIV)**

> *"Everyone who calls on the name of the LORD will be saved."*
> **Joel 2:32A (NIV)**

New Testament confirmation:

> *"Everyone who calls on the name of the LORD will be saved."*
> **Acts 2:21 & Romans 10:13 (NIV)**

"The next morning I was back on my bed… don't know how I got there, but a new peace had started to settle over me. It would take some time, but God was coming to my rescue. I just knew it!"

Discouragement Sets In!

Ellie knew to leave she would have to settle the debt she had with Adela. She had charged her for everything, absolutely everything! She presented her with a bill many pages long starting when she first walked into the restaurant with Besy. She said she owed her for all the food, all the clothes, all the room and board, all the doctor visits, and all the furniture we had bought. The figure was staggering! It looked hopeless. I told her "Adela, I am going to pay you every penny." The next morning Ellie walked into the restaurant for breakfast and gave Enrico, the cook, her order.

He said to Ellie, "Sorry Ellie, I can't serve you."

"What do you mean you can't serve me? Are we out of food? There was plenty of food in the kitchen last night."

"Ellie, we have plenty of food, but your account is closed for lack of payment. You will have to go somewhere else to eat."

"What are you talking about?" "Come on Enrico quit fooling around and get me some breakfast."

"Ellie, I am not fooling around. That order came straight from Adela and she let me know I better not sneak you any food either. She was really angry and had her bouncers with her who let me know to not give you a thing without her permission."

Ellie was stunned! Not even Adela was this cruel. Or was she? Ellie decided she just wouldn't eat. Well, that didn't last long. Finally she gave in to her cruel task master and told Adela she would keep working. Ellie was discouraged – but not defeated – down but not out. No! Not by any means. She became even more determined. This gal was a fighter and she was not going to give up. Adela's attitude and cruelty were just a setback, not the end of the road.

Monica – My First Angel!
"Advisor" & "Daughter of God"

But God had heard her desperate cry – **"God if you are real get me out of here!"** Soon a new bartender came to work at the club. Her name was Monica and she was somehow different. She seemed sincerely interested in the girls and was becoming a mother figure to them. It was a *God divine appointment* that she came, and Ellie found out later her own teen age daughter was also an indentured courtesan in a town on the coast. Her daughter had been trapped as a runaway; became addicted to drugs – and was selling her body on the streets to pay for her drug habit. A cruel pimp had captured her and later sold her to the madam of a club. Monica was trying to find her. But so far she had not been successful. That practice of sex slave trafficking was all too common. It was again a matter of deceit, coercion, and of course police protection over the brothel. It was always about the money.

Well God had His hand on Ellie and soon Monica was close to Adela, and somehow got a sympathetic ear from her. It is no mistake that two of the English translations for Monica is **"advisor"** and **"daughter of God."** She kept talking to Adela and told her Ellie had been there for over two years and it was time for her to go. If she does not get out soon she will be destroyed in both body and mind through the abuse of men and drugs. Just the hard life they all lived would eventually kill you. That was clear from the many destroyed girls. Life expectancy in the club was short, and Ellie had seen many girls destroyed by the *enslaved life.*

It wasn't long till Adela came to Ellie and said "Ok, you can pay off your debt to me and leave. You will start getting a percentage of all the work you do. In fact, I will hold it out and apply it to your account. You should be out of here within a year." Now that was a miracle!

Ellie was stunned! **No girl had ever been allowed to pay her debt** and leave the club. That was how the club operated, and that was how the club made money. It was all part of the coercion plan. This scripture in Exodus One describes the plight of the Israelites under the cruelty of the Egyptians. But it also clearly describes the plight of girls like Ellie who are forced under a slave task master to work at their whim. To not work as required would bring upon them the cruel whip – even death. Rebellion against the taskmasters was met with the cruelest punishment and tortures. If for no other reason to show by example that you are someone else's property till you die!

> *"So they organized them into work gangs*
> *and put them to hard labor under gang-foremen.*
> *They made them miserable with hard labor* – mak-
> *ing bricks and mortar and back-breaking*
> *work in the fields.*
> *They piled on the work, crushing them under the*
> *cruel workload."*

Exodus 1:11-14, *selected parts* **(The Message)**

It was not until years later that Ellie found out the literal translation of the name Monica was "advisor" and "daughter of God." Monica was certainly a gift and advisor from God to the sweet Ellie. Monica's ability to talk to Adela was nothing short of super natural. Her stance for Ellie paved the way for her debt to be paid and her freedom to be won! Our Father God was indeed working through the angel Monica!

> *"Are not all angels ministering spirits sent to*
> *serve those who inherit salvation?"*
> **Hebrews 1:14 (NIV)**

> *"Do not forget to entertain strangers,*
> *for by doing so some people have entertained*
> *angels without knowing it."*
> **Hebrews 13:2 (NIV)**

> *"The angel of the lord encamps around those who*
> *fear him, and he delivers them"*
> **Psalms 34:7 (NIV)**

Years later Ellie would know that the moment she cried out to God angels had been sent to work on her behalf. No doubt,

Monica was one of them and the first one Ellie knew, but she would not be the last.

"You are Free"

It was almost a year before her debt was paid. Adela kept her word and released Ellie, telling her **"you are free."** Ellie was so excited, yet also sad, as she knew she was the first girl in the history of the club to be set free. What about all the other girls? What will happen to them? She knew her good friend Rubia, the Lady Blanca was no longer pretty. Her face was puffy and her belly was extended from fluid buildup. She had a gray color and was constantly in pain from her stomach. No one knew what was wrong, but they had seen the symptoms with other girls as well. Later Ellie would guess that Rubia had AIDS as did many of the other girls. At that time no one called it AIDS, but regardless it was ugly – and it was deadly!

Ellie and Rubia wept together as Ellie said her final goodbyes. It was one of Ellie's hardest and saddest days. Ellie was so excited about leaving, but she was concerned for Rubia and did not want to leave her. Rubia was the only girl Ellie would ever call friend in the club. The club's atmosphere was certainly not conducive to friendships. Rather, it was about survival. And with few exceptions, it was every girl for herself. So the girls saw many come and go, and never knew what happened to them. Some, like the sick ones, were probably turned out on the street to fend for themselves, while others were sold. No one knew for sure!

'Stockholm Syndrome"

It is a known fact that sometimes prisoners are scared to leave the prison, because they don't know what is on the other side of the wall. The reasoning is that the hell that is known is safer than the hell lurking on the other side of the wall. That has been known as the "Stockholm Syndrome." One definition of this syndrome is *"when the captor becomes the person in control of the captive's basic needs for survival and even the victim's life itself. The captive victim judges it safer to align with the task master than to resist and face the consequences, either real or imagined."* In this case the perception is just as real as the reality.

The devil, who hates us and wants to destroy us will do all that he can to convince us that we are okay where we are, and that it would be more dangerous to change or move. But that is a lie and it is coming from the father of lies.

Jesus made it very clear when He gave us these two scriptures!

> *"You belong to your Father, the devil, and you*
> *want to carry out your father's desire.*
> *He was a murderer from the beginning, not*
> *holding to the truth,*
> *For there is no truth in him.*
> *When he lies, he speaks his native language, for*
> *he is a liar and the father of lies."*
> **John 8:44 (NIV)**

> *"The thief (devil) comes only to steal and kill and*
> *destroy."*
> **John 10:10a (NIV)**

Ellie was not going to believe that lie even for a moment. She was taking her hard earned freedom and she was going to walk into her destiny. Little did she know our Father God had a great plan and purpose for her life, and He was moving her into her destiny according to the truth in Jeremiah.

> *"For I know the plans I have for you," declares the LORD,*
> *"plans to prosper you and not to harm you, plans to give you*
> *hope and a future."*
> **Jeremiah 29:11 (NIV)**

"Then will the eyes of the blind
be opened
and the ears of the deaf unstopped.

Then will the lame leap like a deer,
and the mute tongues shout for joy.
Water will gush forth
in the wilderness
and streams in the desert.

The burning sand will become a pool,
the thirsty ground bubbling springs.
In the haunts where jackals once lay,
grass and reeds and papyrus
will grow."

Isaiah 35:5-7 (NIV)

CHAPTER 5

Freedom!

God's favor continued to shine on Ellie as Monica invited her to stay in her modest home till Ellie could get ready for her trip to America. Without Monica's invitation Ellie could have again ended up on the street trying to survive. Ellie had been really frugal over the last year. Not only had she paid off Adela, but she had hidden away $800.

That would give her enough money to get a bus out of Honduras – through Mexico – and into America. She also with Monica's help had gotten her passport – so she was almost ready to go!

Another Heartbreak!

There was still an issue Ellie wanted to take care of before leaving the country. She doubted she would ever return once she left. Her mom was the issue – or the person – that she wanted peace about. More than anything she wanted her mother's love and to understand why her mother arranged a marriage with the insane Miguel. It had been over three years since she had seen any of her family, and the last time with her mother was not pleasant. She had left with her husband Miguel from the government building and had not seen or talked to her mother since. Of course, to travel to her home town was dangerous, as she was still legally married to Miguel; and if he saw her he could force her to return to his little corner of hell.

Her desire to see her mom was more powerful than her fear, and she made the trip. It was one of those sweltering days when you felt like even the shade was on fire as the bus pulled into town. At first Ellie was too afraid to get off for fear of Miguel. But she boldly decided, if she could survive three years in the club, then she would figure a way to avoid him. Besides, she still had her knife and was not afraid to use it!

She got off and cautiously headed for her mom's house. It still looked the same. Nothing had changed. Some of the flowers Ellie had planted almost four years before were flourishing. The flowers made Ellie smile as she and her mom had struggled trying to get them to survive with so many kids running around the yard. There were no kids around today as Ellie approached the door and softly knocked. Her mother soon opened the door and greeted her by saying, "Hey Ellie, good news, you are free."

That was a strange greeting. Not, "Oh, I am so glad to see you, my daughter is home safe." No, none of those words of love.

Ellie said, "I know mom; I settled my debt with Adela."

"Who is Adela," her mom asked? "You are free because your husband Miguel was killed in a car wreck and you are no longer bound to him."

Ellie was flabbergasted. She knew then her mom didn't even know where she had been for over three years. Ellie asked her mom "Were you not even concerned for me all these years. **Why did you not come, look for me, and visit your daughter. I needed you and you were never there!**" Again Ellie felt like the talons of the vultures were tearing at her heart, and ripping little pieces of her soul from her. She had to hold her head in her hands to keep it from exploding. She didn't know which worse – the pain in her head – or the pain in her heart.

Wounded People always wound other people, And usually the ones they love!

The meeting was not good as Ellie realized that her mom was so guilt ridden that to even see Ellie was painful. Her mom reacted as so many wounded and hurting people do, and the reaction is to *bite the person who loves you and needs you.* **Wounded people always wound other people.** At the time, Ellie did not understand that reality – either emotionally or spiritually – so the pain was very deep. Her pain can be described as a *deep inner core pain*, and only God's love can remove that pain. In time, the love of Jesus and the Father God who loves the orphans and fatherless would heal her broken heart! But it would still be years later – after much torment – before she found that peace!

Many years later, Ellie and her husband Randy would return to her hometown in Honduras. Their goal was to locate Ellie's mother to try and share the love they had found with the Lord Jesus and each other. Ellie only wanted to love on her mother, knowing that she had been a victim herself. After quite a search, she located her family – only to learn her mother had died the year before. Ellie was devastated, but knew in her heart she had done all she could do. It was a deeply emotional time as Ellie was reunited with other family members and they were delighted to learn how God had worked in her life.

The Journey

The time spent at Monica's was restful and healing after living for over three years at the whims of different predators. Her days were filled with plans and thoughts about what she would do once she entered America – the land of paradise. Ellie loved to walk and she was finally comfortable walking alone, but she was still cautious. Her street smarts told her to keep the eyes in the back of her head open and wary of any man. Her aunt had told her during her visit to her home village that her older sister had gone to America and was living in the Los Angeles area doing well. That would give her a contact and a place to start with her new life. A new life was what she wanted and she was determined to be successful. She could do nothing about her mother, so she would move on with her life making the best of what lay ahead. Determination was a key word in Ellie's life and it was her tenacity that kept her moving forward to success. She determined that she was not going to be a victim, but rather the victor!

There was an inherent heart-hardening cynicism that long ago stopped Ellie from believing in fair play. But now she was able to better protect herself, and even though her formal education was not advanced, her life skills were acute for a gal her age. That is what the hard life under a task master will do for you. She was mentally quick and could size up people with her clever, well developed mind. Ellie often stated to Monica, "Yes, I can do it. I am going to make it. I have walked though mine fields of depravity and manipulation, but the best is yet to come!"

The time finally came for her to board the bus for California. It was an exciting day. Although there was some sadness that things had not worked out with her mother, she was delighted to leave the environment which had caused her so much pain during her 19 years. She and Monica had a meal together in a nice restaurant and Monica made sure that Ellie was on the bus safely. She gave her a lot of motherly advice – hide your money – watch what you eat – who you talk to – keep your determination on your goal!

The trip distance by bus was approximately 2,800 miles depending on which route the bus took. Ellie had booked the economy fare so it took a couple days to get half way which was Mexico City. They first had to travel through Guatemala, which was no problem, as all they required was a passport. The scenery was fascinating as it kept changing regularly. Ellie had never been far from her home and she had never been out of Honduras. Reality was that most Hondurans never get a chance to see anything other than Honduras, so she felt pretty lucky. Things were changing – she just knew it!

Lourdes – My Second Angel
"Miracles of Healing"

As the bus rambled through the valley of Anahuae, approaching Mexico City, Ellie sensed that something special was awaiting her. The city was enormous! It seemed to stretch from the east to the west and north to south as far as you could see. Teeming masses of people were everywhere and the smog was stifling. They finally pulled into the bus stop and the driver told them they would not be there long; so get refreshed and re-board the bus. Ellie did and quickly was back in her seat ready to leave, when she noticed a kind looking woman in the seat next to her. The bus was not full so it was a little surprising the woman had not chosen to sit by herself as most people had done.

The woman asked Ellie where she was going and where had she come from. The woman then startled Ellie when she said she also was traveling from Honduras on this same bus coming from a visit with her family.

That was an intriguing statement as *Ellie had not seen her on the bus and they had been traveling for two days!*

Introductions were made and Ellie asked her about her name. Lourdes explained that her name was originally French, being so named after a famous pilgrimage site known for its supposedly miraculous cures for the sick. Ellie enjoyed this woman's company and felt comfortable in her presence. During the next two days of travel, they ate all their meals together and Lourdes listened kindly as Ellie shared her life struggles with her. Just sharing with someone who obviously cared was comforting and Ellie's spirit was again soaring that she had made the right decision to go to America. Lourdes was going to be able to help in many ways, and she was familiar with the whole Los Angeles area.

Belly of the Bus

During their talks, Lourdes realized that even though Ellie had her passport she was lacking some other papers, probably a visa, which was going to prevent her from crossing the border into the United States. They were coming near to a town by the name of Creel when Lourdes asked the bus driver to pull over in a rest area as she needed some papers from her suitcase;

which was in the luggage compartment under the large bus. Lourdes seemed to know the bus driver as he quickly did as he was asked. Before stopping, she told Ellie "You are going to have to hide in the luggage compartment or you risk being arrested in this town. Don't worry you will only have to stay under there for about thirty minutes. The officials in this town are known for catching young girls without proper papers and selling them into the same human trafficking you were just delivered from." That was all Ellie needed to hear; and besides she had grown to trust Lourdes, so into the luggage compartment she went. Not only into the compartment, but luggage was removed and she had to hide behind it. She was about five feet from the door behind the luggage. It was claustrophobic for sure, extremely hot, and smelled of diesel fuel, but better than the possibility of being sold again.

It was a long thirty minutes, and sure enough the authorities checked over the bus carefully, but they did not pull out the luggage to discover Ellie behind it. Ellie could hear them talking and moving stuff around, but they never saw her. Again she prayed **"God if you are real get me out of here."** Well she was becoming more and more a believer as she was delivered from the '**Belly of the Bus**!'

Coyote Crossing!

After that experience I knew I could trust Lourdes to keep her word. She had an uncanny ability to know what was going on and how to deal with it. Since I trusted her, I was not overcome when she told me that I was going to have to stay in Tijuana for a couple of days before I could safely cross the border. She had to make arrangements and would not see me again until I had crossed the border with the Coyotes. Coyote is a term used for someone who smuggles a person across the border from one country to another illegally.

Ellie went to the address she had been given and after being questioned and paying them $500 she was allowed into the

Coyote hideout. The place was full of men with only a couple of older women present. She had to walk across a foyer in front of all these men and she told me, "As I walked across the room I felt about as safe as a piece of raw meat in a kennel of mad dogs. This was for sure a scary looking bunch – far worse than any I saw at the club. I was worried, but was confident if anyone tried to touch me or rob me they were going to experience the cold steel of my knife that I had gotten at the club. I was too close to let some man mess up my plans!"

"Actually, they were all very polite and were also just trying to cross the border. At 2:30 in the morning, we left for the trip across country on foot. There were about 20 of us altogether; so they divided us up and we traveled in groups of about 5 per group."

"It was scary! We had to belly crawl on the ground for long distances and we had heard stories the night before of people who had died after being bitten by scorpions and rattlesnakes. Then we had to cross some water that was almost up to my chest. It was pitch black dark and really eerie. But we made it, and as Lourdes promised, she met me at the designated time and place. I was relived and delighted to see her. She and Monica were the only two people I had ever dealt with that had been honest. It was getting better and better!"

Water was gushing forth in her Wilderness and streams were flowing in Ellie's desert!

"Nothing too Difficult"

Behold I will do something new
Like a stream in the desert
I'll amaze you!
My child, look to Me and
rely on my power
Watch and see all I do this very hour!

There is nothing too difficult,
Nothing impossible for Me!

I am near and I have heard you,
I am here and how I long to
Answer the cries of your heart,
Answer the cries of your heart

Cause there is nothing too difficult,
Nothing impossible, nothing too
difficult for Me

Song written by Kathi Wilson
Living Water Productions, LLC
www.Living-Water-Productions.com

CHAPTER 6

"The Promised Land"

"It was unbelievable! I was in the Promised Land. I really didn't know what I was going to do, but one thing I knew for sure – I was no longer a slave in the club. This was a brand new beginning of a whole new life. The joy of my freedom was indescribable. I could already feel the defilement of the last years was being completely scrubbed off me. I still did not have a personal relationship with God through His son Jesus – but I knew when I prayed that night in the club that my Father God had heard, and He had moved on my behalf. There were going to be many more struggles as I worked to come to grips with the programming of my past, but I was not giving up. Life was too precious. And mine was just starting!"

"My angel Lourdes had already been at work on my behalf, lining up a job for me to house sit in a luxury mansion home in the Bel Air section of Los Angeles near Beverly Hills. Having spent my youth as a peasant in a rural village I found these luxury estate houses and gardens to be fancy and plush beyond all I could imagine. There was a gardener at the home who was Mexican and he spoke perfect English. We agreed that anytime we spoke it would be in English so I could quickly learn the language. I knew learning English was going to be very important to flourishing in my new home. He was an excellent teacher never allowing me to flow over into Spanish when I was confused. Instead, he would patiently wait until I figured it out. I sometimes got frustrated with him and with English, but it worked, and my English started coming along strong."

It was not long till Ellie enrolled to learn nails and hair styling and soon after she had her own business. It started out small three days per week at local swap meets where people came to buy and sell; people loved her work and she was making money and getting ahead. Ellie was very industrious and also went to work for the May Company

72

(now Macy's, Inc.), a large department store. Her first job at May was in the restaurant as a dishwasher in the basement. Management quickly saw that she was diligent and understood the application of make-up, so they promoted her to the cosmetics department. Of course, with the promotion came a nice raise and she was able to go to school and obtain her GED certificate. Her diligence was paying off.

During this time she met a charming man and they started dating. Ellie was still trying to overcome all the hatred, anger, fear, violence, and confusion of men which had been ingrained into her life, but Al seemed like a nice kind man. Unfortunately, when you are still trying to cover up pain and bad memories, you often fall into many substitutes for true peace and that is what happened. Al and Ellie did a lot of partying, but even then Ellie was still busy completing her requirements for being a hair stylist. Soon she had completed all the requirements and had all the proper licenses to operate. She was now in business!

Also during this time, President Reagan declared an amnesty for illegal immigrants who were working and going to school. Ellie qualified, and soon she was entirely legal as a permanent resident and on her way to being approved for citizenship. She worked hard and soon was a US citizen. That was a proud day!

Another disappointment!

Ellie's marriage to Al seemed to center around all the wrong things. They lived in an atmosphere of work and party, which is all too often normal for most people. The slogan was: "Just live the good life." Al traveled frequently on his job and during one trip to the Dominican Republic he called Ellie and told her that he had married another woman who lived there, and he would not be back. Wow! That was a shock that caught her totally off guard. Once again, a man had – used her – betrayed her – and left her.

All the past hurts of betrayal, abuse, rejection,

abandonment, shame and guilt came flooding back in and sent Ellie into a tailspin. The tailspin resulted in trying to find comfort in all the wrong places and wrong things. Even during these difficult times, Ellie remembered clearly a *still small voice* that seemed to be talking to her with words of love and encouragement. But at that point, the deep inner core pain was stronger than any other presence in her life. She would understand later that she was actually in a fierce spiritual battle with the father of lies, the evil one, who was trying to take her life. But the enemy would lose and her Father God would win!

"What are you doing? I am your Father!"

The despair of being rejected and humiliated again was almost unbearable. The parties raged and the blur of life was reeling in all the corners of Ellie's life. She would never forget the night God miraculously touched her life again – and it changed her forever!

Ellie tells the story. "It was the weekend and many people were partying at my house – yet nothing seemed right – it was a buildup of impaired confusion and I felt like the wheels were coming off the train wreck of my life. I was very aware that the demonic vultures were again attacking me. I felt like I was trying to tear their talons out of my brain and heart – but with no success. The more I tried to yank the talons out they would sink deeper still. The talons would not come out, instead they sank deeper and the demonic vultures laughed at my pitiful efforts."

"It got worse! Suddenly, I heard a weird hissing sound and looked toward the commotion. There was a large anaconda snake that had just lunged at a rat the size of a small dog. The snake had the rat clamped tightly in its jaws. But it was only the lower half as the upper half was gone – already eaten – by the anaconda! That was exactly how I felt! I was only half alive and almost consumed. Would this be my end? Half eaten by a killer snake or having my heart and brains torn out by vultures? These *apparitions* seemed real and the terror I felt froze my blood and took my breath away!"

"Then I clearly heard these words. *'Ellie what are you doing? I am your Father!'* Instantly, I was sober and in my right mind. Although I did not understand it, I knew the vultures and the anaconda snake were not real. I also knew – yes, really knew – the voice I heard was real. It was soothing, but it was also terrifying, in a different way. I knew it was God! I knew it was the same God who had rescued me from the club and delivered me from the grip of Adela."

In response to the voice of God, Ellie immediately made everyone leave the apartment. She then proceeded to pour out or flush any substance that was left behind by the visitors. Now what do I do thought Ellie. It was so quiet in the apartment. It was nerve racking – a striking contrast to all the noise of the party. It made her anxious and fidgety. She felt she was supposed to do something in response to God's voice – but what?

Pastor Jack Hayford

Just to have some noise in the apartment Ellie turned on the television and then went to the kitchen to fix something to eat, as she was suddenly famished. She was not really paying attention to the TV, it was just background noise. She brought her coffee and sandwich and sat down in the room just as she heard these words, "If you don't know God through Jesus Christ, then today is your opportunity to meet Him." Ellie thought, I was just asking God to show me who He really is. I wanted to hear more. Excitement flooded her and suddenly the food held little interest as she was glued to Pastor Jack Hayford's words being broadcast on a show called *"Living Way."*

"I knew that God was speaking to me. Yes! He was speaking to me as if I was the only person in the world. I had never watched religious TV, but I was mesmerized and started weeping softly as I listened to these quiet gentle words. What was it about this man? He was like no man I had ever heard. But then I had never heard a preacher before – this was a first. Then I knew what it was that held be riveted to the words coming off the screen. This man, Pastor Jack Hayford, believed what he was saying. I was hanging on every word!"

A Mighty Conversion!

The end of the hour long message was being wrapped up when Pastor Jack said, "What is holding you back? Is it the pain from deep wounds in your life? Are you heartbroken because you never knew your father? Is your shame and guilt bigger than the freedom of our Lord Jesus? Are you reluctant to follow the King? No one will ever love you like our Jesus, who gave His life for you. He died that you might have His peace and serve Him – the King of Kings."

"At that moment I felt like Pastor Jack and I were the only two people on the planet. He knew and understood my pain. He also knew and understood that the wheels of my life were running me off the cliff."

"He then quoted this scripture verse from the bible which I had never heard."

**"For God so loved the world that He gave His one and only son,
that whoever believes in Him shall not perish, but have eternal life."**

John 3:16 (NIV)

The words were on the screen and Ellie read them over and over – *'gave His one and only Son'* – *'shall not perish'* – *'have eternal life!'* Precious words that seemed unbelievable to a tormented devastated gal who was losing all hope! But in that moment Ellie knew that an eternal love had gripped her! God was holding her in His arms!

Ellie found herself on her knees as Pastor Jack led her in a simple prayer to receive the Lord Jesus as Savior and Lord of her life. Wow! Peace truly came in and she felt as if she was lifted to another dimension.

God had set her up

Ellie quickly wrote down the name of the church and realized that it was literally within a few minutes walking distance of her home. Unbelievable! *"Church on the Way"* was right around the corner; and the TV speaker Pastor Jack Hayford was the pastor. The church was so close, and it had been there all along – she just didn't know it. God had known it all along, and He knew all of this was going to happen – **God had set her up!** "I knew this **set up** was His love for me," Ellie said. "I was learning there are no mistakes in God and His love for me had been there all along, even as the word declared – it had been there for me before the very foundation of the world. Yes, for me, Ellie!"

"Long before God laid down earth's foundations,
He had us in mind, had settled on us as the focus of
His love, to be made whole and holy by His love.

Long, long ago He decided to adopt us into His
family through Jesus Christ. What pleasure He
took in planning this! He wanted us to enter into
the celebration of His lavish gift-giving by the
hand of His beloved Son."

Ephesians 1:3-5 (MSG)

We are the focus of His love!

Oh dear reader, if only we could get hold of this truth ... *We are the focus of His love!* Having this truth deep in our hearts and minds would transform all we are, all we do and all we think. Our spirit, soul and body would reflect a new dimension of life which is actually supernatural. Yes! We would be radically transformed. Ellie was on the road to this wonderful understanding, but there was still a process taking place to deal with all the hurt and programming of her life.

Ellie was programmed through her life experiences to believe all men were basically predators and liars. *She had never known a man who was trustworthy or safe*; she had been repeatedly abused emotionally, sexually and physically. When these defilements have been your life experience it programmes you to believe lies. It is simply a matter of the lies becoming truth to the victim. What were the lies Ellie had heard and learned? Some of the programming was that all men were self centered, violent, cruel, deviate, abusers, narcissist, and haters of women – only seeing women as objects of their own lust – not concerned for the woman – neither her life nor her dignity. She was programmed through multiple bad experiences to see herself as an object, not as the **focus of His love**. On the other hand, a child raised and trained with God fearing parents will teach a child they are dearly loved and accepted – not only by the parents, but by God as well!

So how was Ellie raised? Let's look at her experiences to see the reality of how she was programmed and taught to believe lies.

- Her mother would take her for a while, but then send her back to the grandmother when it was not convenient to have her.
- Her mother never showed Ellie real love.
- She never knew her real father – not even his name.

- She never knew her grandfather.
- Her step father sexually abused her by the age of 13.
- Her step brother sexually abused her at the same time – in the same house.

- Her friend's uncle raped her when she was 14.

- Her husband (remember she was forced into the marriage) who was more than twice her age was a sadistic alcoholic who sexually abused her and regularly tied her up and beat her for his perverted pleasure.

- Adela, the brothel madam coerced, lied, deceived and manipulated Ellie into a horrible life for three years.

- During those three years she was abused and used by many cruel men.

- The police who were supposed to protect Ellie were vicious and lecherous.

- Her second husband Al was an adulterer and abandoned Ellie for another woman.

- Three men she met and dated in church turned out to be basically phony, and had many hidden secrets about their lives.

What else could this dear gal believe other than all men were just like the ones she had known – bad! Just plain bad! When you never experience a good man over your whole life you are now *programmed to believe the lie* – in this case the lie was that all men are BAD!

Lies Become Strongholds

Strongholds are one of the enemy's favorite weapons against all humanity. The devil knows if he can build **Strongholds** in our lives, we will become ineffective and powerless in our Christian walk. **Strongholds** can keep you from yielding your life to the Lord Jesus; and those same **Strongholds** can maintain a constant dark cloud over your life that serves as a veil to conceal and hide the truth. **Strongholds** can actually cripple a person as it causes torment and destruction in both the mind and the body. The wicked one, satan, knows he can win the spiritual battle with the Saints if he can *control or program the mind*. It all starts in the mind!

This little chart shows how subtle the programming progression of a **Stronghold** is:

- ➤ #1 - It starts with *Deception* which is *Hearing* the Lie
- ➤ #2 - It becomes a *Foothold* which is *Listening* to the Lie
- ➤ #3 - A full blown *Stronghold* is formed as you *Believe* the Lie

The story of Adam and Eve (Genesis Chapters 2 & 3) listening to the devil and falling into sin by *choosing* to disobey God is a clear illustration showing this destructive pattern which is still in operation today!

How do you change?

You start the change by acknowledging that you have a new leader in your life through the your new birth. Your new leader is also your Lord and Savior and He desires for you to learn all about Him and His ways. Jesus said:

> *"I am the way and the truth and the life. No one comes to the Father except through me."*
> **John 14:6 (NIV)**

Well, if that is true – and it is – then you must study and follow *"the way, the truth and the life."* The only way to do this is by spending time with your new Savior and with other people who love and serve Him as well. In other words, you become His disciple and fellowship with other disciples. His life will start manifesting through your life as you draw closer to Him and His truth.

Ellie would have many more divine appointments, revealing that God's love focus was on her life as He set her up. In Part Two we will see how God revealed His love and purpose through a myriad of people. These people included the pornography king Larry Flint as she ministered to him as a hair stylist – the TV personality Nancy O'Dell, the recent star of NBC's show Access Hollywood – and her dear husband Pastor Randy Collins – the man in whom she found true love and safety. But first let's look at some areas that are pertinent to our healing and deliverance from the programming of our past abuses and defilements.

"I Hung On To My Cross And Not Offenses"

"I hung on to my cross and not offenses.
I despised shame and rejection for love!
Follow me in my example,
Verily, you will be free!

So let go of every hurt and transgression,
Bitterness and resentment, too!
Hang on to your cross and not offenses,
And my healing love will flow to you!

Chorus:
It's up to you to be free or bound
It's up to you to be free or bound.
I hung on My cross and not offenses

Will you hang on to your cross or offenses?
Will you forgive when you have done nothing wrong?
Will you hang on to your cross or to your offenses?
It's up to you to be free or to be bound.

I denied myself instead of you!
It was love personified!
I picked up my cross and not offenses;
It was great love for you that I died!

Chorus:
It's up to you to be free or bound.
It's up to you to be free or bound.
I hung on to My cross and not offenses."

Song written and performed by Deanne Day
Copyright Deanne Day
www.RestoringHearts.net
All Rights Reserved

Walk through memory lane

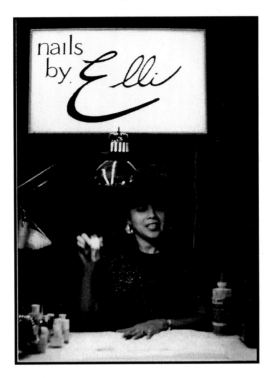

Ellie's first job in America!

Ellie sang in a church choir
before meeting Randy

The Love of her life...

I DO!!!

Always singing!!

1998 - Church on the Way

**Trip to Hondurus
to find
her
family**

2007 - Vacation Cruise

where she is today...

Singing and teaching at The Rock of Anaheim in California

Part 2

RESOLUTION & RESTORATION

CHAPTER 1

"A Ministry Letter"

I recently had a discussion with a lady I was ministering to that had issues similar to Ellie's. Although not as extreme or long term, she too had been sexually abused and was struggling with the after-effects of programming. Fear, rejection, betrayal and other similar issues had her bound. She was being tormented and often found herself in the midst of full blown panic attacks. She had been told by a well meaning minister that if she was *born again* then all the junk would fall away. The minister was using II Corinthians 5:17 as the basis for the teaching that once you are born again – all is ok. What does II Corinthians say? Let's look at it.

"Therefore, if anyone is in Christ, he is a new creature; the old has gone, the new has come!" (**NIV**)

Now it definitely says the old is gone and the new has come. But there is a problem. So let's address that problem. In order to understand the issues here, I want to quote a letter I wrote regarding this subject – and the whole subject of old wounds. I believe this letter clarifies much of what Ellie came to understand as she was working through her issues. These scriptural principles are not just theory – they are life changing dynamics that will also change your life and help you to redeem others from the pit of hell.

The Letter

Greetings Dear Saint!

Beloved, you are a Saint! And the simple understanding of who you are is often the Alpha and Omega – beginning and the end – of all true healing and restoration! We must see ourselves as He sees us; and He sees us as complete in Him and His righteousness. That is a Saint! The apostle Paul never wrote to the sinners. No, he wrote to the Saints! Were they perfect? No! But they were Saints because of His sacrifice and His work on the cross. Not your hard work or good deeds – no, it was His work alone that brought you into His presence and His grace. Settle that once and for all – as many people try really hard to save themselves or deliver themselves – but it is all about Him. Yes, it is all about Him!

Remember the important scripture from Ephesians 1:3-5: *He had us in mind. He had settled on us as the focus of His love, and He took pleasure in planning us.* Wow! I just love being the *focus of His love*. You too, dear one, must come to know you are the *focus of his love.* Yes you are! You, beloved, are the *focus of His love!* Come on; keep speaking the word to yourself that you are *the focus of His love!*

You have asked a very important question and one that has caused some confusion in the body of Christ. For that reason, I want to try and share my heart with you and what I have learned over many years of **R**estoration ministry. I have seen countless people set free, delivered, healed, restored and running after the vision and destiny God has for them. Our Father God also has a powerful vision and destiny for you and you will find it as you step into His truth.

Ellie did it and she is free! You can do it to!

The answer lies in what we call the Restoration **R's.**

The Restoration **R**'s are:

> ➢ **R**evelation

> ➢ **R**edemption

> ➢ **R**esolution

> ➢ **R**estoration of **R**elationships …. God, Self & Others

> ➢ **R**evival

We will look at these in a little more detail ….. not necessarily in this order.

We have seen the truth established over and over. The truth or the revelation is that much sickness, torment, and dis-ease come from one of three major relationship areas in our life. These areas can be found in the words of Jesus to the lawyer in Mark 12:28-31 (NIV)

One of the teachers of the law came and
heard them debating.
Noticing that Jesus had given them a good
answer, he asked him.
"Of all the commandments, which is the
most important?"
"The most important one" answered Jesus, "Is this:
Hear, O Israel, the Lord our God, the Lord is one.
Love the Lord your God with all your heart and
with all your soul and with all your mind and
with all your strength.
The second is this: Love you neighbor as yourself.
There is no commandment greater than these."

I have repeatedly and consistently found over many years of ministry that if one of these areas is out of sync with God's purposes for your life, then all kinds of junk comes floating our way. Refer to my book "Life in the Red Zone" www.RestroingHearts.net for a more detailed understanding.

What are the three areas? The answer lies in these relationships ….

1 - Relationship with <u>God</u>!
2 - Relationship with <u>Others</u> or our Neighbor!
3 - Relationship with <u>Our Self</u>!

Recently, I was teaching a conference regarding these truths in a large church and some folks got healed just sitting in the congregation as they got *their thinking in line with God's thinking.* They were healed before the team ever laid hands on them. *God just moved on them as the revelation truth of dealing with broken relationships became a reality to them.*

Ok, Saint, back to your question of who is right? Is the minister who says *to not dig up old decayed things,* or the minister who testified and led ministry around *issues of inner healing, because of old decayed things?*

Well the answer is, they are both right! But there are really two different issues. The wicked one has successfully kept us from dealing with these issues due to our lack of understanding of inner healing – or wounds of the soul – a deep inner core pain.

First, we must define healing or restoration. I define healing and restoration as the point in time when there is *no longer any pain in the memory*! The memory will probably always be there, but the pain can and will be gone. Now that is good news! An example would be if and when someone thinks about the person or persons that offended them, and along with the thought, they get a certain 'ping' or ache in their gut – or they feel their blood pressure rising – or they feel their face flush

– then *they have not been healed* of that offense. More work needs to be done!

Ellie gets no more 'pings' from her past abuses! And you too can be 'ping' free!

I personally do not like the term *inner healing* as there has been considerable confusion, and at times, even harm to the body of Christ due to the lack of understanding as to what the real inner healing is. There are also occasions where people associate *inner healing* with some esoterically new age goobeldy gock. For that reason, we have chosen to use the term **Restoring the Heart, www.RestoringHearts.net**, as this is more applicable and descriptive in the present spiritual arena, particularly in the western church.

Why is the one minister right about not digging up old decayed things? We have witnessed on too many occasions where well meaning zealous folks, but spiritually ignorant, have tried to assist people in digging up old decayed things; and the exercise ended up being disastrous. It is not just digging up an old decayed thing that is the answer. Most of us know the junk embedded in our souls, which we refer to as *deep inner core pain.*

Many dear ones are tormented spirit, soul and body, as they constantly dig up old decayed things, but with no **R**esolution. Till there is **R**esolution in the **R**elationship issue the wicked one comes along and uses what we know as accusing spirits, which are actually evil spirits, to condemn us and tell us all kinds of junk about how we are – *no good – never amount to anything – you are a dirty rotten sinner – God loves everyone but you –* and on and on the accusing voices run their filthy mouth! They love to tell countless lies about us, as well as to us, in order to sabotage the precious deep work of the cross in our lives.

Remember, we showed the evil demented progression is from – deception – to foothold – to stronghold! The enemy's goal is to get you in his strongholds where he can destroy you. This is the work of the enemy and he has 6,000 years of human history under his belt and he knows through our personal history – as well as our generational history and sins – what 'buttons' to push to bring us under conflict and condemnation. The enemy cannot read our minds. However, he can see how we react to certain situations and he can hear the words out of our mouth (Death and Life are in the power of the tongue – Proverbs 18:21) and then use our own words and actions to kill us. Yes, he wants to kill you. Make no mistake – the enemy's desire is to destroy you!

The wicked one tried to kill Ellie, but he FAILED and she is free!

In my own testimony, (you can read it in "The Warrior's Walk") I tell the story of while serving in the Marine Corps I got a gal pregnant and helped her to get an abortion. At the time, I thought it was no big deal, but through the years, it became a *really big deal* as I was tormented about the abortion by accusing spirits. It is important to know that after I got born again and filled with the Spirit I was *still never free from the torment* of the accusing spirits of condemnation. I had confessed the sin many times and repented of it countless times – yet still relief was only temporary at best. There was no **R**esolution!

Why was I not free? Dear one, if you are reading this and not free then God is giving you a divine moment to find freedom – as Ellie did and as I did. Remember ***"God is no respecter of persons"*** (Acts 10:34). He does not show partiality. What He does for one, He wants to do for the other. If you need His touch, then open your heart to His love and allow His grace to flow in! He wants to flood you with His love.

The answer to why we are not free is usually very simple. The answer is found in **RESOLUTION!** Yes, just **R**esolution of the old decayed things that God puts His finger on. You see, He has for years been trying to put His finger on the issue – which is the **Revelation** – while at the same time, the enemy was busy putting condemnation on you.

That beloved, is spiritual warfare and we often are losing the battles for lack of knowledge of what the spiritual warfare is. Let's look at scriptures in both the Old and New Testaments to highlight and confirm that spiritual knowledge is indeed important in our spiritual walk.

"My people are destroyed for lack of knowledge."
Hosea 4:6 (AMP)

"Therefore My people go into captivity to their enemies without knowing it and because they have no knowledge of God. And their honorable men are famished, and the common people are parched with thirst."
Isaiah 5:13 (AMP)

"To keep satan from getting the advantage over us; for we are not ignorant of his wiles and intentions"

The Apostle Paul speaking to the Corinthian Church
II Corinthians 2:11

The church has often stood firm and been able to cast out demons as Jesus commanded us to do. However, we have been woefully lacking in seeing ourselves free by the precious blood of Jesus. Yes! He has provided for our freedom. We often just don't believe it. It seems too good and too easy to be true for us. It is true for Ellie, but me Lord? Lord, **can** you really do it for me? Lord, **will** you do it for me? The Lord is crying out to you **YES!** I can and will do it for you. It is yours! Take it! The Lord is loudly saying Remember; *you are the focus of My love*! Yes you!

We must come to the place where we know who we are in Him, and not believe the lies that the enemy has told us over and over.

Ellie got her freedom and she wants you to have it! Take it!

You see it is often just not as simple as *casting out demons and laying hands on the sick.* God certainly uses that all the time, **BUT, IF** there is an unresolved issue of deep inner core pain and it is not dealt with through **R**edemptive **R**esolution then the healing or deliverance will only be temporary as satan still has a legal Stronghold in our life!

The lack of **R**edemptive **R**esolution is the reason that just a small percentage of people are healed or delivered in the typical prayer line!

Ok, let' look at the major issue that will keep us in bondage!

One of Ellie's big Revelations is coming up!

A STORY ABOUT FORGIVENESS

*At that time Peter got up the nerve to ask,
"Master, how many times do I forgive a brother
or sister who hurts me? Seven?"*

*Jesus replied, "Seven! Hardly. Try seventy times
seven.*

*"The kingdom of God is like a king who decided
to square accounts with his servants. As he got
under way, one servant was brought before him
who had run up a debt of a hundred thousand
dollars. He couldn't pay up, so the king ordered
the man, along with his wife, children, and
goods, to be auctioned off at the slave market.*

*The poor wretch threw himself at the king's feet
and begged, 'Give me a chance and I'll pay it all
back.' Touched by his pleas, the king let him off,
erasing the debt.*

*The servant was no sooner out of the room
when he came upon one of his fellow servants
who owed him ten dollars. He seized him by the
throat and demanded. 'Pay up. Now!*

*The poor wretch threw himself down and begged,
'Give me a chance and I'll pay it back.' But he
wouldn't do it. He had him arrested and put in
jail until the debt was paid. When the other servants saw this going on, they were outraged and*

brought a detailed report to the king.

The king summoned the man and said, 'You evil servant! I forgave you your entire debt when you begged me for mercy. Shouldn't you be compelled to be merciful to your fellow servant who asked for mercy?' The king was furious and put the screws to him until he paid back his entire debt. And that is exactly what my Father in heaven is going to do to each of you who doesn't forgive unconditionally anyone who asks for mercy."

Matthew 18:21-35 (MSG)

CHAPTER 2

Forgiveness – the Key to Liberty

Every time I read this scripture about the king, and his servant who would not forgive, I find a Godly fear of the Lord comes on me. And Godly fear is a good thing. This scripture is God speaking directly to us about how important He considers forgiveness. We need to constantly be reminded that often our thinking is not in line with our Lord's thinking. When that is the case, our thinking becomes a great big **IF**.

An example of an **IF** would be when someone comes for prayer for an issue which resulted in bitterness and unforgiveness. Let's say it is toward a father – mother – brother – sister – spouse, they will not get healed or delivered till they get **R**esolution of the issue! In these cases **R**esolution will only come when they decide to be obedient and follow the heart of God and *forgive* their offender. If they are holding on to an offense, and not willing to forgive, they have become a captive in prison. And only they have the key to the prison door. Forgiveness is the key to the prison door!

In Ellie's situation numerous offenders had to be forgiven!

But Ellie forgave and she is free!

We have seen literally thousands of people healed and delivered of all sorts of dis-ease, torments and emotional trauma when they chose to line up their thinking with God's thinking. When you line up your thinking with His thinking, then Forgiveness and Repentance naturally, or shall we say supernaturally, will follow! Jesus was the only normal man who ever lived because He always did what He saw and what He heard the Father do or say. And He always forgave – setting the normal example – for us to follow. This is what should be defined as the normal Christian life, but often we find deep wells and pits of *unforgiveness, bitterness, anger, shame, guilt, rejection, self hatred, abandonment, strife, anxiety, fear and unconfessed sin* – just to name a few of the sin issues keeping us from living the normal Christian life. All of these issues become great big **IF's** in our life and result in never being free from the results! You must find the **R**esolution. Till you find the Resolution you will still have pain that will paralyze areas of your life. It becomes a pain that paralyzes!

Cause and Effect is inexorable

Remember the law of cause and effect is inexorable. **IF** we don't deal with the cause – we **WILL** suffer the effect. It is just a matter of time. All of these issues we just listed are the **IF causes** – the sickness, torment and dis-ease are the **effects**! This may seem harsh to some, but it is none the less true. *God will not heal you, or free you from your torment, and let you keep your sin or issue!* Yikes! Ouch! To some that is a painful reality. But we need to get a hold on this reality. Sometimes it is so hard for us to let go of issues because often they have become a part of our personality through the years of programming. But let go we must, **IF** we want to be free.

Part of the **R**evelation is this reality – you cannot stand at an altar and say, "Lord please heal my bad liver." And yet keep drinking a fifth of whiskey each day. Yes, God in His great mercy can indeed miraculously heal your liver – **BUT IF** you keep guzzling that fifth of whiskey like a crazy movie cowboy – you might as well buy a nice pair of boots to be buried in! Cause boot hill – here you come!

An 'Anorexic' healed

Recently we ministered to a woman who was anorexic. Through ministry, we got to the root cause or the **IF** of her deep inner core pain and dealt with it through **R**edemptive **R**esolution and **R**epentance and she was delivered and healed! She is now eating and looking in the mirror. Before her healing, she would not even look at herself in the mirror. Now she looks and sees a Saint of the most-high God who is loved, treasured and has great value to her Savior and husband Jesus. She now sees herself as *the focus of His love* and His love is the reality of who she is! Not who she thought she was! She now understands and believes that her *identity* comes from what God says about her – not what someone else said about her. The stronghold of a false *identity* has been replaced by the reality of her true *identity* – which is *the focus of His love*!

In ministry, we know *behavior tells you what you believe about yourself*. For instance – not eating because you think you are fat – or eating too much for comfort – or cutting yourself – or drinking and drugging into oblivion – or other self destructive behaviors. Now when you get the **R**evelation of who you are in Christ, and your true identity is in Him, then your *belief about yourself determines your behavior*. Do you see the difference? One is life and one is death!

Her healing and deliverance was particularly exciting as we found out for thirty years she had been prayed for many times without results – in many churches – anointed with oil, but when she dealt with **R**elationship issues around her family – daddy – tons of abuse – mother, more abuse – multiple marriages and other broken **R**elationships with friends and family, she was healed and delivered. She got the **R**evelation and she followed the obedient path of her Lord Jesus. This path took her through a quick process of **R**edemptive **R**esolution and **R**econciliation, and now she is living in **R**evival! A powerful testimony!

Ok, Lord that sounds good – but how do I get it? Well, you get the **R**evelation that it is for you! What is for you? His peace is for you – the same peace He promised us in Isaiah 53:5 and John 14:27.

"He was pierced for our transgressions,
He was crushed for our iniquities;
The punishment that brought us <u>peace</u> was upon
Him,
and by His wounds we are healed."
Isaiah 53:5 (NIV)

<u>Peace</u> I leave with you;
My <u>peace</u> I give you. I do not give to you as the world
gives.
Do not let your heart be troubled and do not be afraid."
Jesus words in John 14:27 (NIV)

Ellie has Her <u>peace</u>, but it took time on the battlefield!

So you see, the other minister is also right. We have to deal with those old decayed things if they have not been dealt with and brought to a **R**edemptive **R**esolution. Now the word **R**edemptive is very important here. In fact, it is crucial to our freedom, deliverance and healing. It always comes back to His blood shed for us on the cross. What Jesus did for us we cannot do for ourselves and it is **R**edemptive.

Often ministers, friends and family will try to get you to dig up old decayed stuff – but just digging it up and talking it through is not always **R**edemptive. This is not a mind game – trying to see a situation a certain way – but a truth issue! Yes, our mind has to be renewed with the truth. And He – the Lord Jesus – is the truth according to these scriptures. **R**estoration has to involve having the mind of Christ.

"Do not be conformed to this world (this age),
(fashioned after and adapted to its external,
superficial customs), but be transformed (changed)
by the (entire) renewal of your mind (by its new
ideals and its new attitude), so that you may
prove (for yourselves) what is the good and
acceptable and perfect will of God, even the thing

*which is good and acceptable and perfect
(in His sight for you)."*
Romans 12:2 (AMP)

*"If you stick with this, living out what I tell
you, you are my disciples for sure. Then you will
experience for yourselves the truth, and the truth
will set you free."*
John 8:32 (MSG)

You see, for any modality of **R**estoration healing to have effective results, there has to be **R**esolution. And often the **R**esolution requires Forgiveness and Repentance. Any modality of spiritual and scriptural healing that does not bring you to a place of Forgiveness and Repentance needs to be questioned. Not all, but certainly most issues have to be brought to a place of **R**edemptive **R**esolution.

The one minister you mentioned testifies of his year's long struggle with depression and heaviness of heart. He finally got the deliverance he had been asking for when he got the **R**evelation and the **R**esolution. Even after the **R**esolution, he had to struggle against the programming resulting from a familiar spirit flowing through his generational family curses.

Before we continue with this ministry letter, lets look at another startling testimony from our dear Ellie!

Larry Flint, Porn King

Ellie, through her tenacious determination, quickly ascended in the hairstyling world of the Hollywood celebrities. She owned her own shop and worked for the salons that were sought after by the glamorous Hollywood crowd. She would often make house calls as some of the stars were very private and avoided the paparazzi. Larry Flint was one of those celebrities who had Ellie come to his ultra luxury home or his publishing office building on Rodeo Drive.

A little history on Larry. On March 6, 1978, Larry and his lawyer were shot outside the courthouse in Guinnett County, Georgia where he was on trial relating to an obscenity charge. The shot resulted in permanent spinal cord damage paralyzing Larry and placing him in a wheelchair. Larry's personal life is one of tragedy, and unfortunately he has made untold millions of dollars in hard core porn and the gross exploitation of many women.

Ellie had been styling Larry's hair not knowing his history or what he stood for. One day, as she was shaving his neck with a straight razor, Ellie realized the depth of his involvement in pornography!

Ellie said, "Fury rose up in me toward this man who represented all the things used against me sexually that had tried to destroy me. The fury was like a burning flame of defiling hate and all within me wanted to cut his throat – right then and there. It was all I could do to suppress my feelings and emotions and I almost ran from the building. I was furious! I was mad at him – I was mad at God for allowing me in his place – I was mad at myself for my uncontrolled emotions – hey, I was a Christian now and this fury was not supposed to be happening. All the old bad memories of the club and my two abusive husbands came flooding back into my mind. I was worried I was going to lose my mind through the released fury. I was shaking so badly I could hardly drive. I finally had to pull over as I was afraid I was going to have a wreck."

"O God what am I going to do?" She cried. "I thought I was past all of this." The same loving Father God who rescued her from the club and had brought her this far again answered in His still voice saying ***"Go to church – there is something special for you there tonight."*** Ellie said she argued with God saying, "But I don't want to go and I don't feel like going!" But to church she went out of obedience to her Father God. She was learning to trust His still small voice!

Another Set Up

Ellie got to the church and found she was still so frustrated she could hardly sit still. Her mind was in a thousand places – none of them good! But God was there and **He had set her up.**

There was a visiting speaker and when he got up he said, "I used to work for Larry Flint of Hustler Magazine selling millions of dollars of pornographic materials. I was making a pile of money until one night in a hotel room in New York City I happened to turn on the TV to a preacher named James Robinson and I got saved. Yes, I was born again and gave my life to Jesus watching the TV. I immediately got out of the porn business and God is continuing to clean me up from the inside out."

Ellie was stunned! Absolutely stunned! Is this possible? After just today finding out who Larry Flint was and fleeing in anger – because he represents the degradation of women and all she detests in her experience with men. The man went on and said "Don't ever give up on anybody. You never know what is really going on in their life or in their heart. Just look at me as an example." He said, "I was making tons of money working in a defiling business, but God, in His mercy, redeemed me and He can redeem anybody. Don't give up!"

The speaker continued and said that God had shown him sin was sin, whether it was porn or something else. He reminded the audience that anything short of the glory of God was still sin, quoting the scripture in Romans 3:23.

"For all have sinned and come short of the glory of God."

Ellie's anger was instantly gone – replaced by the deep knowledge that she was the *focus of His love*. What a set up! Only an all knowing – all powerful – all loving God could have pulled this off! All the planning in the world could not have pulled this off. The only word to describe it was *supernaturally unbelievable*. To think, the very day Ellie was styling Larry's hair and realized what he did and then to have an ex employee come to her church – one of thousands in the area – to share that he had worked for Larry and he had been saved, through a TV preacher. Wow, Ellie had also been born again while listening to a TV preacher. Really it is absolutely unbelievable all the coincidences which had to happen for God to perform this *Set Up*. But this set up was just a taste of how much God loves Ellie and how much He loves you!

Ellie knows she is the focus of His love – Do you believe it yet?

Remember, if Larry Flint's employee can be brought to God through Jesus Christ then so can Larry. Pray for Larry. Ellie prays for him and hopes to give him a copy of this book as a testimony of what God did in her life. She actually worked for him almost four years and although she detested what he stood for, she found him to be gracious and soft spoken. God has His hand on Larry as He does on everyone else who needs to know they are the *focus of His love*, even in their issues!

Don't forget, the Bible is full of men and women who were sinners doing 'gross stuff' and yet, God had His hand on them. Men such as King David who was a manipulator – an adulterer – a murderer and a liar, not to mention he stood on his rooftop and watched Bathsheba bathe. The term for this behavior today is *Voyeurism*. In clinical psychology, voyeurism is defined "as the sexual interest in or practice of spying on people engaged in intimate behaviors, such as undressing, sexual activity, or other activity usually considered to be of a private nature." Well, by today's terms that could easily relate to pornography. So was there hope for King David? Yes! God loved him and delivered him. Ok, is their hope for Larry Flint? Yes of course! God is no respecter of people and He loves Larry just as much as he loved King David and wants to bring him into His kingdom!

Never forget that God, through Jesus Christ, died on the cross, taking the sins of every man, woman and child! *However, we must appropriate His love by responding to His love through agreement with Him and following Him!*

Nancy O'Dell a delightful client – one of many!

Ellie had many clients who were well known in this star studded area of California. Her reputation as a top notch stylist was also well known, bringing her in contact with many of the celebrity stars. Even though Ellie and Randy now live far from the Hollywood scene, she is still pals with a number of these sweet folks.

Nancy O'Dell is one of her delightful friends. You may know Nancy as the star of NBC's *"Access Hollywood"* or the *"Dateline NBC"* Show. Nancy is also known for her work with the Muscular Dystrophy Association and as the National ALS Ambassador. Ellie is still in touch with Nancy as their friendship was more than just professional.

Paul Grace – My Third Angel
A Financial Miracle

Ellie experienced many, many miracles along the road to her freedom and we have already looked at Monica – the bartender whose love helped release her from the club. And we saw the angel Lourdes – the woman who helped her across the many days of bus travel as well as delivering her from the belly of the bus. She then got Ellie into the United States, setting her up with a good job to help establish her dignity and learn English.

So who was Paul Grace? And why was he an angel? Following Ellie's conversion and journey towards wholeness in body, soul and spirit, she attended church regularly and was hungry for the word of God, knowing that the *"truth would set her free."* She had already come into understanding that the word of God – Jesus's words to the people – and the words of the apostles such as Paul, Peter, James and John would transform her life. This scripture from John 8:32 in The Message Bible defines it clearly.

> ***"Then Jesus turned to the Jews who had claimed to believe in Him. "If you stick with this, living out what I tell you, you are my disciples for sure. Then you will experience for yourselves the truth, and the truth will free you."***

Ellie, being the attractive engaging gal she is, had no trouble making friends and she was often asked out by men in the church. Unfortunately however, she quickly learned the truth that church attendance did not equal holy attitudes or behavior. Consequently, she had some bad experiences with careless damaged men, and was therefore leery of them when they wanted to get closer. She understood quickly that just because a man was in church did not mean he had her best interest in mind! So naturally when Paul Grace approached her with questions about where she lived and how did she like her apartment and even asked about the cost of her apartment – she immediately became suspicious – thinking ok, what does he really want?

Her street smarts were kicking in and she was alert for the punch line as he told her she could purchase a $250,000 luxury condominium for only $50,000! Would you believe a story like that? Of course not. I know I wouldn't believe it. There has to be a catch or trick somewhere! She was even nervous about going to see this condominium with Paul alone, so she got one of her gal pals and they went to see it. They were shocked! The condo was unbelievable and was in a beautiful upscale section – obviously worth more than the $250,000. Ok, what is the catch? There wasn't one! Ellie was not sure what all the legal jargon was, but it was some kind of repossessions deal. But, if the deal was that good then Paul Grace would have bought it and resold it for a major profit. After all, wise real estate agents do that for themselves when they find a deal saving $200,000! Why would he do it for a stranger? Because he was an angel!

Bottom line was Ellie and Paul soon met with a banker, and Ellie proved she could afford the payments on a $50,000 mortgage. After signing the papers she was now a proud home owner.

Why do we say Monica, Lourdes and Paul Grace were angels? Monica was so completely different from any bartender in the club and somehow got Adela's ear on behalf of Ellie. Remember Lourdes had helped Ellie, and even stayed in her home for a few days prior to going to work in the mansion. Some time later Ellie went to Lourde's house to see her and let her know she was doing well – but Lourdes was not there and no one had ever heard of her! And the same thing happened with Paul Grace. Months later she went to thank him and no one knew who he was!

God again showed Ellie she was the focus of His love!

Let's continue now with the 'ministry letter' …..

'MERCY REIGNS'

*My God is strong enough to raise me
from the grave
Your love is great enough to take away
my shame
My God is making new, the wreckage of
my heart
Your hand is reaching down, to pull
me from the dark*

*Your mercy reigns, Your mercy covers me
Your grace sustains, Your grace is all I need*

*Your Spirit is my strength to
overcome the past
I set my eyes on You,
and find a grace that lasts*

*Your mercy reigns, Your mercy covers me
Your grace sustains, Your grace is all I need*

*I'm forgiven, washed inside a
love that never lets go
You never let go*

**Song written and performed by:
Chris Brown, Mack Brock & Wade Joye
Elevation Worship Publishing
www.Elevationworship.com
All Rights Reserved**

CHAPTER 3

Ministry Letter continued ...

How did I get free from the torment of the abortion I was party to? Remember, I had repented countless times over the years, and I still was not free. The enemy used to love to bring the abortion issues to my mind as I was ministering from the pulpit, or in a counseling session. That tactic was really *yucky*. Remember, this is spiritual warfare and the enemy does not play fair. He wants to steal, kill and destroy us and he does not give up easily. He knows there is too much at stake. He wants you bound so you cannot function as a spiritual warrior. He may have lost you to heaven, but he will destroy your peace or your testimony in order to sidetrack the kingdom work in you!

Ok, so how did I get free? One day I received the **R**evelation that I was washed by the blood of the Lamb and my past sins had no control over me as I walk in His victory. I suddenly realized this precious truth.

> *"He takes our sin as far away as the east is from the west" and "He remembers our sins no more"*
>
> **Psalm 103:12, Jeremiah 31:34b & Isaiah 43:25**

You see, I understood this intellectually and could teach it, but I struggled with the thought that perhaps my sin was too big. I should have known better – after all I was raised in church – and had gone to the altar at a Billy Graham crusade at a young age to give my life to Jesus! These were not conscious thoughts, but rather unconscious thoughts running around deep inside my mind to torment me and keep me off spiritual balance. Of course it was foolish and wrong thinking, but the perception often becomes the reality and again the enemy can be masterful in making the perception so strong.

Wow! It hit me one day! God in His sovereignty had

110

decided when we confess our sins He is faithful to forgive – it is just that simple. As I John 1:9 says,

"If we confess our sins, He is faithful and just and will forgive us our sins and purify us from all unrighteousness" (NIV)

In other words, God made a decision – declaring that when we agree (confess) with Him about our sin issues, He *forgets the sin as if it never happened!* Dear one, your sin which has been confessed and repented of is gone. Yes gone! It is no longer on your rap sheet! It is gone – gone – gone! Why dig it up if it is gone?

Now that was a **R**evelation to me. I saw for years that I had been crying out for forgiveness and God didn't even have a record anywhere of the abortion or all the other yucky stuff I had done. No! *He chose to forget it*, so why I am thinking about it and letting it torment me? The **R**evelation came to me that I didn't believe God was honest when He said He **Forgave and Forgot** my sin. Whoops! So then I had to repent for not believing His word!

The Battlefield

Sometimes it takes time to work through the issues needing **R**estoration. It was true for Ellie and it was true for me. It will probably be true for you as well. However, the victory is worth the battle, so don't run from the battlefield. Be a Warrior and run to the sound of battle! Get in the fight!

How did Ellie come through the battle? First, she didn't shy away from the fight. She wanted to be free and the battle was worth it. She knew the years of abuse were going to take some time to work through – but work through them she did! She was fortunate that in her church, where she was born again, there was offered a **R**estoration modality of healing called *Cleansing Streams.* She did not give up or give in, but worked her way through this program three separate times – each time finding more freedom.

Today she is a major part of the Restoration ministry called *Redeeming the Time,* developed by her husband, Pastor Randy, and used to train disciples in an intense 12 week study course, culminating with a retreat. They have been doing this for a number of years and have trained well over 1,000 people in this ministry. The testimonies coming out of this training are phenomenal!

I have been blessed that our team at Restoring Hearts Ministries has worked closely and in partnership with Pastor Randy and Ellie in bringing **R**estoration too many.

You see, as long as the sin of abortion was hanging around unresolved, I had terrible issues of shame – guilt – rejection – mad at myself – self hatred – because I was a failure, and the enemy just loved my dilemma. My lack of knowledge was destroying me, but the **R**evelation came and I was set free! Now I, along with Ellie, have seen multitudes set free from the same issues.

A Larger Issue – Sins done to us!

Ok, we have looked at issues caused by our own sin, but our experience reveals a much larger issue – the **sins done to us.** This is a major issue and I have found most Christians, as well as people in general, have unresolved issues in their life from when they were wounded or sinned against by other people. This is very damaging, and even more so when the victim is young and does not know how to deal with the wounding – whether it is physical, sexual, emotional or spiritual. This is when the wound quickly becomes a *deep inner core pain* which will fester and destroy the victim if there is not **R**edemptive **R**esolution.

We looked at II Corinthians 5:17 which said: *"That when we are in Christ old things are passed away, all things made new."* Well, now that is true once you have the **R**esolution of the old things. But, **IF** someone still hates their father – mother – brother – sister – coach – teacher – previous spouse – former friend – or themselves, then they are being tormented as they have not agreed with God and His word concerning Forgiveness and Repentance! The ministry of **R**estoration is always an ongoing ministry. It is not something you get once and never have to deal with again. Certainly an individual, by the power and grace of God, can be set free instantly (as we have seen in alcohol or drug addictions) but an ongoing **R**estoration discipleship agenda is needed to continue to grow in grace. Even when there is an instant healing or deliverance, there also needs to be ministry dealing with the IF's behind the addictions, wounding and other unresolved issues opening the door for the wicked one to torment and harass you. It could best be described as the process of sanctification.

Sanctification

A good definition of sanctification would be *"the state of being set apart from the secular and sinful, unto a sacred purpose. This sacred purpose would be to be conformed to the image of Christ and to reveal Him to the world."*

It is a process and **R**estoration ministry is a vital dimension of the process. For instance, if you have been the victim of someone else's sin, as Ellie was, then sanctification requires you come to a place where you can *forgive*! Is it easy? No, but it is necessary to follow Him and be part of His supernatural love and mercy. People often ask "How could Jesus forgive those who mocked Him, beat Him, put a crown of thorns on His head and finally crucified Him?" The answer is He did it because His Father said to do so! It really is just that simple. Well, if Jesus did it for His Father – because forgiving love was His Father's nature – then how can we do less? We can't do less and expect to grow in grace and manifest His love to a broken world!

In fact, if we don't forgive we can expect to stay prison

captives as was described in the Matthew 18 chapter. Your freedom, as well as your families' (verse 25), may well depend on your willingness to walk on the battlefield and fight till the victory is established. Again, get in the fight!

Ellie "Forgave" and got the victory – You can too!

Crohn's Disease healed

In closing this letter, I want to share with you two testimonies confirming the truths of what I have been sharing about **R**esolution and **R**estoration. The first one was from Bill Johnson, pastor of Bethel Church in Redding, California. Pastor Bill related a story of a woman who came through a prayer line for healing of Crohn's Disease. Crohn's Disease is defined as a form of inflammatory bowel disease and the exact cause is unknown. The symptoms are ugly, including persistent watery diarrhea, fever, fatigue, loss of appetite and weight, and sometimes severe abdominal pain. There is no known cure! And people suffering from Crohn's also suffer sometimes from hopelessness and despair. But our Lord Jesus is the great physician and He can cure Crohn's Disease or any other.

When the lady got to Pastor Bill and told him her condition, He prayed, as he knew this was possibly terminal, and the Lord gave him a ***word of knowledge***. Pastor Bill did not have the answer, but he knew the Spirit of God did as revealed in First Corinthians.

"But to each one is given the manifestation of the Spirit
for the common good.
For to one is given the word of wisdom through the
Spirit, and to another the <u>word of knowledge</u> according
to the same Spirit; to another faith by the same Spirit
and to another gifts of healing by the one Spirit,
And to another the effecting of miracles, and to another
prophesy, and to another the distinguishing of spirits,
to another various kinds of tongues, and to another the

interpretation of tongues.
But one and the same Spirit works all these things,
distributing to each one individually just as He wills.
For even as the body is one and yet has many members,
and all the members of the body, though they are many,
are one body, so also is Christ."

I Corinthians 12:7-12 (NAS)

He then repeated what he had heard the Lord say to him by asking her, "Do you have any shame over a forgiven situation from your past?" "Yes I do," she said as she started crying. Bill then responded. "*Confess* your shame – as the sacrifice of Jesus was sufficient for your sin and shame – *Repent* of the shame and God will heal your body." She did as Bill asked; and God did indeed heal her of the Crohn's Disease. You see the issue here was a big **IF** in her life. She got the **R**evelation the **IF** was her shame for a past sin which she had already confessed and she got the **R**esolution when she *Repented* of the shame! What followed was the healing and the **R**evival! Pastor Bill never even knew what the shame was all about, but she knew, and God knew. Then she lined her thinking up with God's thinking and the **IF** was **R**esolved and she was healed. Now that is *good news*!

The Healing of Mrs. California

I love the story of Mrs. California's healing from the disease of Fibromyalgia. Tonda, my son Joseph and I were attending a Christian Booksellers Association convention, when God arranged a divine appointment with Mrs. California. She was there as a Christian speaker and author. We met her in the convention hall and after some polite chit chat, she asked me if I had any success praying for people with Fibromyalgia. Through ministry experience, we did know Fibromyalgia is often caused by a big **IF** in someone's life – usually associated with bitterness, fear and unforgiveness – often toward a father or other important male figure. Often this is the case, but not always.

Fibromyalgia is a nasty condition marked by long-term, body wide pain and tender points in joints, muscles, tendons, and other soft tissues. Fibromyalgia has been linked to fatigue, morning stiffness, sleep problems, headaches, numbness in hands or feet, depression and anxiety. The medical community has recognized traumas – physical or emotional – as playing a role in the development of this syndrome. But with that understanding, they still consider it etiology unknown, meaning they don't know the cause or the cure. But, our God knows the cause and He knows the CURE!

The Red Zone!

We explained to her the effects of living in the Red Zone and the issues causing the torment. Again, **R**estoration ministry has revealed repeatedly the issues of bitterness – fear – shame – guilt – self hatred – rejection and abandonment can and will place you in the Red Zone. Further, you will stay in the Red Zone till you get **R**esolution of the issue which started the downward slide into torment and disease!

In the simplest terms, the Red Zone is what the medical community calls the *resistance stage of fight or flight.* In the resistance stage, your body is pumping excess amounts of adrenaline and cortisol which will destroy the 'T' cells and the 'B' cells of your body. Since your 'T' cells and 'B' cells are main components of your immune system, you can predict your immune system is going to break down under the excess amounts of the heavy chemical load. *It is not a matter of if it will break down, but when*!

"Up jumped the rabbit!"

She was a quick learner. We soon were asking her if she had major traumas prior to the onset of the Fibromyalgia, which was now two years old. She explained both her nephew and her father had died within thirty days before the beginning of the disease. She felt the trauma was long gone and she said, "As far as I know, I have no bitterness or unforgiveness towards anyone! I believe I have worked through the issues. It was very difficult as I loved both of them dearly and their deaths were so close together." We continued talking and she suddenly said, "Would it make any difference if my father committed suicide"? A statement like that is what I call an **up jumped the rabbit R**evelation. Now the whole situation changed – he did not just die in his sleep, but rather took his own life! Now the situation of the trauma has dramatically changed.

God immediately gave me a word of knowledge and I asked her, "Have you forgiven your father for taking his own life and depriving you of his love and affection?" She immediately broke down and started weeping. She was overcome with emotion and we had to quickly get her a chair to sit on. I knew at that moment that our Father God, by the Holy Spirit, had given her a **R**evelation of the issue! The **IF** in her life was the bitterness and unforgiveness towards her deceased father, which she had 'stuffed' deep in her soul, so she would not have to deal with the pain of her loss.

What was the issue of her **R**evelation? Well, she was really ticked off and angry at her Dad for taking his life! But remember, she was a devoted Christian, church leader, conference speaker and book author; so she was not supposed to be mad at him. She certainly could not express it to anyone. No! She had to honor her father, even if he had taken his life and she was furious about it. Her idea of honor meant she could not mention she was mad. In her theology, anger at his suicide would not be honoring to her father. In fact, she had never admitted her anger to anyone before telling us. It was too painful. She had to stuff the anger, bitterness and unforgiveness; and it quickly became a *deep inner core pain*. The deep, inner core, soul pain soon became a full blown pain – but now it was flowing outwardly in the form of

Fibromyalgia. What started on the inside was now showing up on the outside. But God loved her dearly, and arranged a divine encounter with folks she did not know to minister to her.

Through her tears and sobs she asked us, "What am I going to do? I see it – I have been wrong to hold on to this and it is tormenting me!" I told her, "We are going to lead you in a simple prayer of forgiving your father and releasing him from his sin. Then you are going to ask our Father God, in Jesus name, to forgive you for your sin issue of unforgiveness, anger and bitterness you have held in your heart toward your dad for two years. And you will ask God to heal you from the effects of the *Red Zone living* and restore your health physically and emotionally."

Well she did as we instructed and was immediately healed as she was sitting in the chair. All the pain left and the heaviness of heart dissipated! Yes, it happened as she was sitting there in the presence of her Father God.

She contacted us two days later and said, "I got back to the hotel and decided not to take my various medications for the Fibromyalgia. I knew in my heart and body God had touched me. *I could actually feel His touch when we prayed!* It has been two days now and I have had no symptoms or problems at all!" We kept up with her and even a year later she was still pain free and off all her meds. Now that is good news!

You see, she got the **R**evelation – which was unforgviness and bitterness towards her dad – then she got the **R**esolution – forgiving her dad and releasing her bitterness – then she got the **R**estoration – healing from God – and finally she got the **R**evival – living free to manifest His glory in the earth!

Ellie wants you to have the Revelation, Resolution, Restoration and Revival!

'Nothing Will I Withhold'

You have poured out Your favor,
You have poured out Your grace
You've changed me by Your unrelenting
passionate gaze
You have called me Beloved,
You have called me Your Bride
And You've shown me I have absolutely
nothing to hide

From You, my Merciful Savior, from You,
my Beautiful King
You have drawn me into Your chambers and
I bring everything
I bring it to You, my Merciful Savior, to You,
My Beautiful King
You have drawn me into Your chambers
and I bring everything

I bring it to You, my Merciful Savior,
to You my Beautiful King
You have drawn me into Your chambers
and I bring everything

Nothing will I withhold, nothing will I withhold,
Nothing will I withhold from You
Nothing will I withhold, nothing will I withhold,
Nothing will I withhold from You

From You, my Merciful Savior, from You,
my Beautiful King
You have drawn me into Your chambers
and I bring everything ...

Song written by Kathi Wilson
Living Water Productions, LLC
www.Living-Water-Productions.com

CHAPTER 4

Randy & Ellie - A True Love Story

Everybody loves a love story. Especially me!

In the world as we know it today, true love is often defined as *one person meeting the needs of another person.* Is that true love? No. It is not, and such a definition reveals the shallowness of what people often think true love is. Ok what is true love? It is the laying down of your life for another as demonstrated by our Lord Jesus when He suffered and died via the crucifixion in order that we may live – and not die. Now that's true love!

> *This is how God showed His love among us: He sent his one and only Son into the world that we might live through Him. This is love: not that we loved God, but that He loved us and sent His Son as an atoning sacrifice for our sins.*

I John 4:9-10 (NIV)

Ellie had never known real or true love till she met Randy – and just meeting him was not enough. In other words, it was not love at first sight, although she felt he was somehow different. She could not put her finger on it, but her discernment was saying, *this guy is different.* Of course, over a number of years, Ellie had emotional experiences with so many damaged and fractured men; it was difficult to believe she would actually meet one who was not consumed with himself. They all talked a good game – but their actions revealed something else entirely. The bible calls our actions and words fruit and teaches us that we can know what is in a person's heart and mind by looking at the fruit of their life. Some have called this *fruit inspecting.* Ellie was learning to be a good fruit inspector!

Today, Ellie teaches other women how to be fruit inspectors. She knows the time it takes to inspect the fruit will save much heartache and emotional torment. She loves these scriptures to show the importance of inspecting the fruit – not just listening to the words. Words can lie, but the fruit will always be real – good or bad – and reveals what and who the person truly is!

"Be wary of false preachers who smile a lot, dripping with practiced sincerity. Chances are they are out to rip you off in some way or other. Don't be impressed with charisma; look for character. Who preachers are is the main thing, not what they say.

A genuine leader will never exploit your emotions or your pocketbook. These diseased trees with their bad apples are going to be chopped down and burned."
Matthew 7:15-20 (MSG)

➢ **Ladies, don't be impressed by a man's position, his car, his wealth, his natural talents or abilities – but study his character. What does he stand for? What does he live for? Who are his friends? What are his intentions toward you? Are they honorable? Is Jesus the Captain of his salvation?**

"If you grow a healthy tree, you will pick healthy fruit. If you grow a diseased tree, you'll pick worm-eaten fruit. The fruit tells you about the tree."
Matthew 12:33 (MSG)

➢ **Ladies, just look and listen. The deep desires of a man's heart will be quickly revealed – look and listen!**

*"You don't get wormy apples off a healthy tree,
nor good apples off a diseased tree. The health
of the apple tells the health of the tree. You must
begin with your own life-giving lives. It's who
you are, not what you say and do, that counts.
<u>Your true being brims over into
true words and deeds."</u>*
Luke 6:43-45 (MSG)

➢ **Ladies, a simple test of fruit is money. What does he
spend his money on? A healthy man is first giving
back to the Lord and to His work!**

*"My friends, this can't go on. A spring doesn't
gush fresh water one day and brackish the next,
does it? Apple trees don't bear strawberries, do
they? Raspberry bushes don't bear apples, do
they? <u>You're not going to dip into a polluted mud
hole and get a cup of clear, cool water, are you?</u>*
James 3:10-12 (MSG)

➢ **Ladies, this one is the 'clincher'. Jesus said if we
are right with Him then out of our lives would flow
"rivers of living water." What flows out of his life –
clean water or dirty water?**

Ellie had heard all the slick lines and seen all the sweet smiles. But under the slick sweet facade was often lurking just another emotionally damaged, self centered, wrong intentioned man just out for what he could get. A church going, hymn singing playboy looking to add notches to his gun belt! Ellie was not interested in being just a notch on some gunslinger's belt. No, she was looking for a man of honor, integrity, and full of the grace of God! Randy was just such a man, but it would take time for the totality of the fruit to be seen.

Ellie was in no hurry. She knew her heavenly Father had picked out the perfect man for her – and He had done it before the foundation of the world.

Ellie had been involved in bible studies while seeking God as a new believer. She was often drawn to the bible stories such as Jacob and Rachel, as described in Genesis 29. She read the thrilling story of Jacob's love for Rachel. Jacob had been smitten by Rachel at the well, to the point of performing a super human feat of removing the stone off the well by himself. Whatever it was about Rachel at the well, young Jacob was suddenly deeply, crazy in love with her. Rachel was the focus of his life and he was supposed to have her for his wife after working for Laban for seven years, but Laban tricked him, and he ended up married to Rachel's sister Leah instead. But he didn't love Leah. He loved Rachel. So again he worked for seven years to marry Rachel – his true love! Ellie knew in her heart she wanted a man who would love her like Jacob loved Rachel – but did such a man exist? She didn't think so. What man would work 14 years to prove his love for you? Certainly not any of the men she had known, including the men she had gotten to know in the church.

But Ellie could see that Randy was such a man, tender, caring and considerate. He was refreshing. All her experiences with men previously had shown that they were all narcissists and completely selfish. The only man who had showed true concern for her was her friend Efrain, at the club, and he had been murdered. The enemy even used his murder to accuse her with the thought – if any man who is decent and caring gets close to you something bad will happen to him and to you!

Principle of Transference

A sad statistic is the divorce rate is just as high in the church as it is in the general population. As a minister, I really struggled with the breakdown of marriages until I received the **R**evelation of the principle of transference. What is the principle of transference? It is the age old principle that people look to and believe that another person can, and will, fill those deep needs in our lives which only the Lord can fill. Whenever we don't trust Jesus to meet our deepest needs, we *transfer* expectations to others, and that is usually our spouse or the ones closest to us. Ministry experience has shown me through the years that most marriages fail because the marriage relationship is built on **vain imaginations, and not reality**! In short order, the vain imaginations get quickly muddled – usually after only weeks or months – and then the relationship really starts falling apart. Sadly, the marriage relationship is already in trouble when the foundation is built on vain imagination!

What's the Rush?

Ellie was in no hurry. She didn't want to be a notch or a statistic. Neither was she just running around looking for a husband. No, she had a husband and his name was Jesus. Sure, she would be thrilled if God brought the right man into her life, but she was going to rest in His love till God moved – not before!

Ellie had seen many of her friends in the salon really tormented by bad choices of the wrong men. She didn't want or need that kind of drama. She had learned through her life experiences that her heavenly Father had only good and perfect intentions toward her, and He was quite capable of taking care of her – husband or no husband!

Ellie was learning she was the focus of His love and she rejoiced to hold on to this scripture in Jeremiah 29 when doubt flooded into her heart and mind.

"This is God's word on the subject: I'll show up and take care of you as I promised and bring you back home (Crossing Over*). I know what I'm doing. I have it all planned out – plans to take care of you, not abandon you, plans to give you the future you hope for."
Jeremiah 29:11 (MSG)

*("Crossing Over") added for emphasis, not actually in the scripture.

"Crossing Over" = Rest!

Yes, Ellie was resting in the reality that God had it all planned out and He only desired the best for her. She had literally *Crossed Over* – she had been delivered from a life of constant physical, emotional and spiritual abuse into a new country with unlimited opportunities and safety. But the true life changing **Crossing Over** was learning that her life, peace, and joy was only to be found as she rested in His arms of safety and love.

It was at this time of learning to rest that Randy came into her life. They were attending the same church and had been involved in some of the same activities. They both loved to sing and often were on the same worship team. In the midst of these activities and bible studies, the Spirit was working on each of them as He had a plan – a plan much bigger and much better than either of them could have ever hoped for. God's plans are always best! Our Father God has written a script for our lives which is much better than anything we could hope for or even dream about. We just need to rest in Him. When you are in God's plan, you have **Crossed Over and you are at Rest!**

Ellie was looking for a special character quality in a man, but she didn't really know how to describe this elusive quality. She just knew when she saw this special character quality – it would be different from anything she had seen in a man. Later, she would know the word she was looking for was *transparent*. Transparent is not a word you often think of when describing someone, but Ellie knew transparency was the key to a Godly relationship. A good definition of transparency in the spiritual sense would be someone who is not trying to hide anything. Their life is an open book – not hiding their issues, past failures or present challenges. In other words, what you see and hear is the real deal. No phony baloney!

True Spiritual Test!

During Ellie's bible study she found what she knew was the true spiritual test to tell if a person was real or phony. Not just for a possible marriage relationship, but this test would also work for any true relationship. Many people had told her they loved God and only wanted to do what He wanted them to do – in the church and in the general public – but the reality was they were living primarily for themselves and would use you and abuse you in a heartbeat. This was confusing to say the least! For Ellie had believed if folks were active in the church then they must be alright. Wrong! She had learned at an early age people are not what they tell you, but she was not expecting the same to be true in the church. She had the false assumption if you are in the church regularly – well, then you must be ok.

As always, the word of God reveals the truth and also gives timely, unchanging principles to live by. In this case I John 1:3-7 (MSG) clearly speaks!

"We saw it, we heard it, and now we're telling you so you can experience it along with us, this experience of communion with the Father and his Son Jesus Christ.

Our motive for writing is simply this: We want you to enjoy this, too. Your joy will double our joy!

> *This, in essence, is the message we heard from Christ and are passing on to you: God is light, pure light; there's not a trace of darkness in him. If we claim that we experience a shared life with Him and continue to stumble around in the dark, we're obviously lying through our teeth – we're not living what we claim. But if we walk in the light, God himself being the light, <u>we also experience a shared life with one another</u>, as the sacrificed blood of Jesus, God's Son, purges all our sin."*

Now it was easy! All Ellie had to do was be ready when a man showed up who walked in the light and did not live in darkness. If and when it happened she would be looking for the real fruit of righteous character and honor. She knew from experience those traits would be revealed – and usually quite soon!

Ellie was really excited about this reality of **walking in the light**. The word was clear – walk in the light – hiding nothing – and you will be in a wonderful experience with God, who is light. Well, if you are in a wonderful experience with God, then all He has to do is connect you with someone else who is also walking in the light with Him. Then the two of you will be walking in the light together! This was almost too easy and too good to be true. But, Ellie was not sure if she had ever met anyone who walked in the light – there seemed to always be some hidden secret or agenda. Her lifelong programming had made her wary and distrustful of men, as well as some women.

Ellie found Randy was the real deal!

Pastor Randy was not a perfect man. In fact, Randy had his own set of issues ingrained in him over life's deep inner core wounds of betrayal, double mindedness, rejection, shame and guilt over relational issues; as well as multiple marriages. Yes, there was some baggage – Randy also had deep issues with trust. He too had been burned emotionally and spiritually – the scars were still fresh – but healing and restoration were taking place.

Behind all the issues however, was a man whose heart was seeking after God. Had he been a proud man? Yes! But Randy had learned that *pride is the treason of a person against the Creator.* He had learned that being self sufficient was to be at enmity against God, for God wanted to reflect His love through us and the manifestation of His love through us will not happen if we are living our own lives – and not His! Randy was coming into the deep revelation that *transparency* was the necessary ingredient for a man to walk with Jesus!

No one would touch their heart!

All the time Ellie and Randy were dealing with their own issues, God was setting them up for each other! The one thing Randy and Ellie had in common when they first met was a pledge **"that no one would touch their heart"**! But their loving heavenly Father was going to reveal His heart in each of their own hearts! He was going to pour His loving grace on them and draw them to Himself – thereby drawing them to each other in His matchless love!

The Set Up!

The script was being written as Randy and Ellie found themselves singing and worshiping the Lord as part of the church. They both loved to sing and their heart was to worship God for His goodness – even in the midst of their individual struggles.

At the same time, they were each busy with their own healing and deliverance from the wounding and heartbreak of their past – some even very recent wounds! Ellie remembers one of her friends at the salon telling her, "Ellie, God has a man picked out for you and you will know him because, when you meet him, he will say something like **I'm home**." Another friend told her "God will tell this special man upon meeting you: ***Ellie, you are going to be my wife!*** Well it all sounded way too strange, but God was at work and that is exactly what happened!

Ellie recalls the day they were singing multiple engagements for the church and had been on their feet for hours at a time. They were resting between the services when the Spirit of God fell on Ellie to pray for Randy. She knew little about him but the Lord spoke in His still small voice and said, "this man loves me – he is mine – I have called him – he is suffering his own inner turmoil because of the 'wounds of a friend' and he needs you to pray for him." The Lord went on to say, "Randy is a brand plucked from the fire and the work I have called him for is just beginning." Ellie did pray for him that day and continued to pray for him daily.

Randy too had been praying for Ellie and one day, as he prayed, the Lord spoke to him saying: ***"Ellie is going to be your wife, now get out of the way let me do the work – Rest in My love!"***

It was some time later that God put the icing on the cake for each of them. Randy was at a men's meeting sharing about the need to be *transparent* when he got a call to come share the same message with a mixed group meeting later that same evening. The meeting was quire a distance away, but e knew he was supposed to go regardless of how tired he was. This was the '**set up**' as God was writing more of the script for Randy and Ellie.

To Randy's surprise, Ellie was at the meeting, but he shared just as openly with this mixed group as he had with the men. Ellie was thrilled. She was touched. She had never heard a man be so honest. This man was willing to share even the deepest struggles of his heart with a mixed group. He hid nothing! And he held nothing back, sharing the good – the bad – and the ugly. Ellie was floored. His testimony – though heartbreaking

– was so refreshing! It was like a cleansing wind was blowing through her soul and refreshing her spirit! She was reminded of the chorus *Come Holy Spirit*. And come He did!

Later, as the meeting was finishing up, Randy walked Ellie to her car. It was a chilly California night and Randy knew that Ellie was cold without a sweater. In a very brotherly act of concern, he put his arm gently around her shoulders and for a reason he did not understand he said: ***"I'm home!"*** That statement melted Ellie's heart and she knew God had spoken to her as she remembered her friend had told her that was exactly what would happen. Some would call it coincidence, but Ellie knew her Father God had spoken to her through one of her friends. Interestingly enough, Ellie also remembered Randy saying to her at one of their first meetings something like "**Someday, you are going to be my wife**", or was it, "**Someday I will have a wife like you Ellie**." Randy was confused as both of these comments were so random. The comments made no sense to him at the time, and actually he was a little embarrassed by the randomness of them. The glory of these comments – that seemed random – was not random at all, but Father God just performing another glorious **set up** for His dear children – Randy and Ellie!

Of course later, the seemingly random comments were known to be a confirmation to both Ellie and Randy. They knew their Father God was faithful and had poured out His love to them very clearly – once again confirming they were *the focus of His love*!

Where are they now?

They are happily married and serving God at "The Rock" Church in Anaheim, California. They were part of the first 150 people who were at this new church and have served in various capacities over the last number of years. Today the church numbers in the thousands and Randy and Ellie are still busy teaching the clear word of Redemption and Restoration.

Multitudes have been set free and established in their walk with God due to the faithful ministry of this dear couple.

Ellie and Randy are free and they are living in the land of joy and delight! Their prayer is for this story of "Crossing Over" to be your story as well!

What would I do without You, Lord?

What would I do without You, Lord?
Where would I be without your love?
All of my strength is from my joy in You
And I am nothing without You Oh Lord

What would I sing if not your praises?
What would I speak if not your Holy Word?
What would I see if not through eyes of faith?
I'd be so blind

Oh Jesus I will praise Your Name forever
And I will lift You up for all the world to see
For you have brought me with a precious price
And willingly I yield
And my life is Yours to do with as You please

So I will sing your praises Lord
All of my days upon this earth
No one can take the hope You've given me
I'll never die because You live in me ... Oh Lord

And Lord I want to live in You forever
Because You are the only life there is to live
Oh Jesus I will follow You
Wherever You may lead
And I'll be with You forever through eternity

What would I do without You Lord?

Written and performed by:
Jan Marie Savoie
Copyright: Jan Marie Savoie
Saugus, Massachusetts

CHAPTER 5

The script continues on ...!

Did we write the whole story? No, the whole story would take volumes. Did we perhaps miss some details of this tragic life turned to a life of His glory? Probably, but the realities of the pain, suffering and torment – replaced by His love, grace and tender mercies is revealed in the daily testimony of Ellie's *Crossing Over*. **The script continues to be written** and the glories yet to come will be greater than the former glories.

Their lives are now an open book for all to see and they are like Paul when he said:

"Your lives are a letter that anyone can read by just looking at you. Christ himself wrote it – not with ink, but with God's living Spirit; not chiseled in stone, but carved into human lives – and we publish it." **II Corinthians 3:2-3 (MSG)**

There is no reality stronger than the testimony of a changed and transformed life. All the words and preaching can become like clanging cymbals, or just noise in your ear. But a transformed life is so radical you have to pay attention. As I have shared Ellie's story in different places it is not uncommon for people to say things such as "if that happened to me I would be in an insane asylum," or "I just couldn't live with all that wounding and hurt." But Ellie is very alive and well and sharing the gospel of Jesus Christ everywhere she goes! She is a living testimony to His love! She knows He has used all those tragedies to give her compassion for others. She is very busy teaching and ministering to others the same love and mercy she has received. She is Restored!

The song *"What would I do without You, Lord"* by Jan Savoie sums up the reality of Ellie's deliverance and daily salvation.

What is that reality? That nothing can be done without the Lord! No, nothing! Yes, many folks can live their lives in their own strength by sheer will power, but soon that strength – your own self determination and strength – will fade, and you are left struggling for the true breath of life. Power and freedom only come by releasing your life into His hands and allowing Him to do as He pleases!

Ellie and Randy's daily cry is like this song...

What would I do without You Lord?
Where would I be without your love?
All of my strength is from my joy in You
And I am nothing without You Oh Lord

Oh Jesus I will praise your Name forever
And I will lift You up for all the world to see
For you have bought me with a precious price
And willingly I yield
And my life is Yours to do with as you please!

Ellie has come to the safe place of knowing she is not her own, but she is bought with a price. She belongs to her Lord Jesus and her desire is to serve Him. And as she serves Him, she is pouring out her life for others, that they too may live and know the same great joy of ***Crossing Over!***

In closing, let's look at an important scripture which reveals what has happened to Ellie and what God desires for you! These promises are for you and your families – take them and tuck them away in your heart. Your Lord is going to show up for you as He did for Ellie – you too are going to have a ***Crossing Over!***

The Spirit of God, the Master, is on me because God

anointed me.
He sent me to preach good news to the poor,
Heal the brokenhearted,
Announce freedom to all captives,
Pardon all prisoners.

God sent me to announce the year of His grace –
A celebration of God's destruction of our enemies –
and to comfort all who mourn,
To care for the needs of all who mourn in Zion,
give them bouquets of roses instead of ashes,
Messages of joy instead of news of doom,
a praising heart instead of a languid spirit.
Rename them "Oaks of Righteousness"
planted by God to display his glory.

They'll rebuild the old ruins,
raise a new city out of the wreckage.
They'll start over on the ruined cities,
take the rubble left behind and make it new.
You'll hire outsiders to herd your flocks
and foreigners to work your fields,
But you'll have the title "Priests of God,"
honored as ministers of our God.
You'll feast on the bounty of nations,
You'll bask in their glory.

Because you got a double dose of trouble
and more than your share of contempt,
Your inheritance in the land will be doubled
and your joy go on forever

Isaiah 61:1-7 (MSG)

Can you hear Ellie shout?
Come with me!

Let me show you the joy
of

Crossing Over!

REFERENCES

If you need ministry in the areas we shared, we have a staff of loving people waiting to help you on your journey to your "freedom."

You can contact us at:

www.RestoringHearts.net

BOOKS AND MATERIAL

If you enjoyed this book, be sure to pick up Ish Paynes other books. Go to www. restoringhearts.net.

The Warrior's Walk

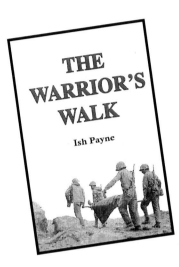

This book parallels the life of a Christian and the life of a marine. In a story-type manner, you will go on a journey with Ish as he scaled walls, ran miles in the rain or cleaned floors. all in preparation to equip him for the real army... God's army... **to FIGHT the good fight of faith."**

The Red Zone

"The Red Zone is a condensed and easy to use handbook that every home should have. From testimony (and humble openness) in his own life and heart, to the corroboration of science with scripture, Ish's joyful and straightforward presentation of the nefarious "red zone" is every man's emergency prevention kit for the number one ailment of postmodern society: STRESS. Now available as a workbook too.. pick up your copy today.